40 Coloring desing for adults

Beach Coloring Book

Thank you for purchase

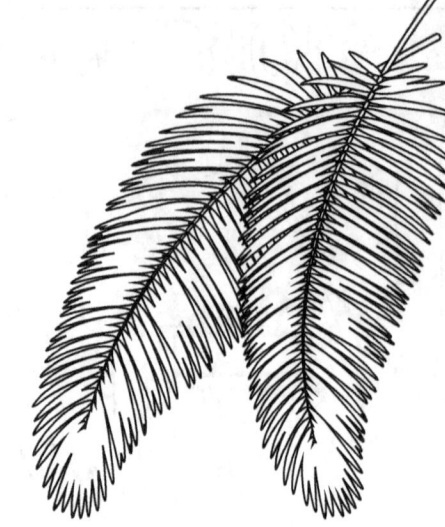

With this adult coloring book you will have hours of creativity, it is the perfect way to relax with the beautiful coastal landscape from the comfort of your home, with a variety of designs ranging from medium skill level to advanced level of complexity.

Have fun painting lovely seascapes, lighthouses, palm trees, sailboats, dreamy oceanfront resorts, and much more!

Ideal for all ages, it's a good and fun way to relax and reduc stress.
To ensure that you have the best experience using this book for coloring and to prevent bleeding, (although the illustrations are printed on one side to prevent bleeding) it is best to color with pencils. If you are going to use another type that may cause pages to bleed, we recommend that you use the buffer page.

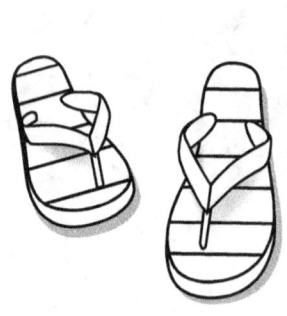 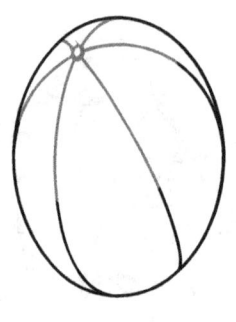 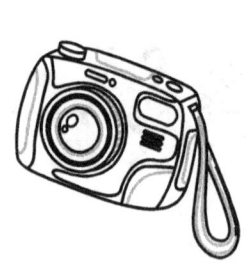 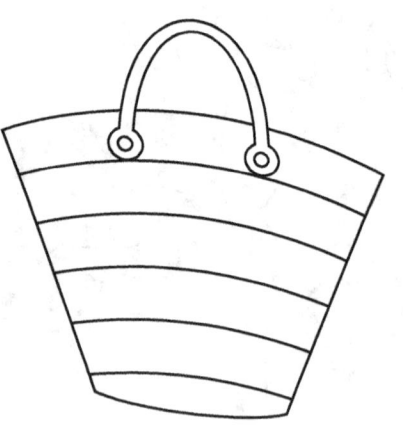

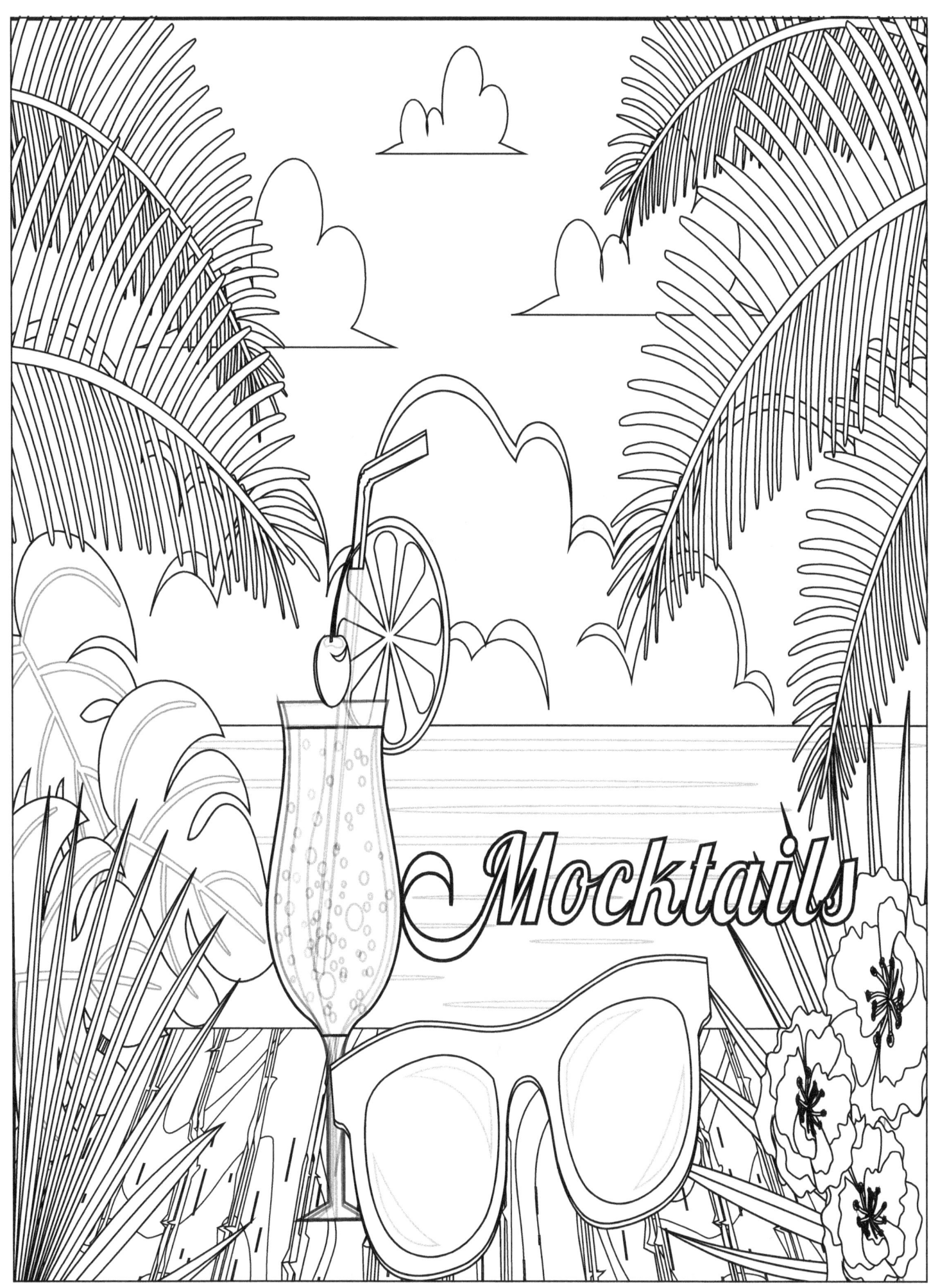

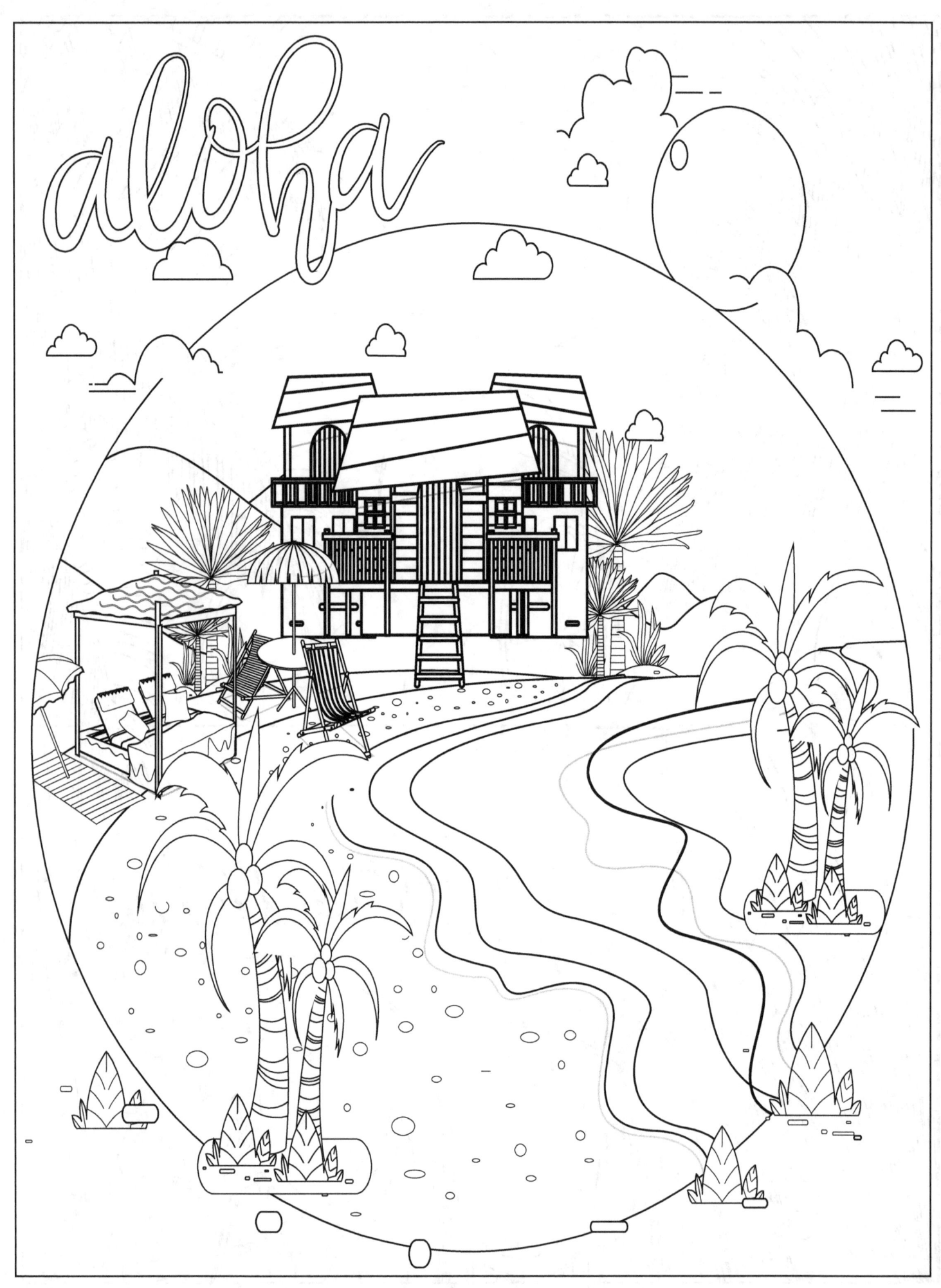

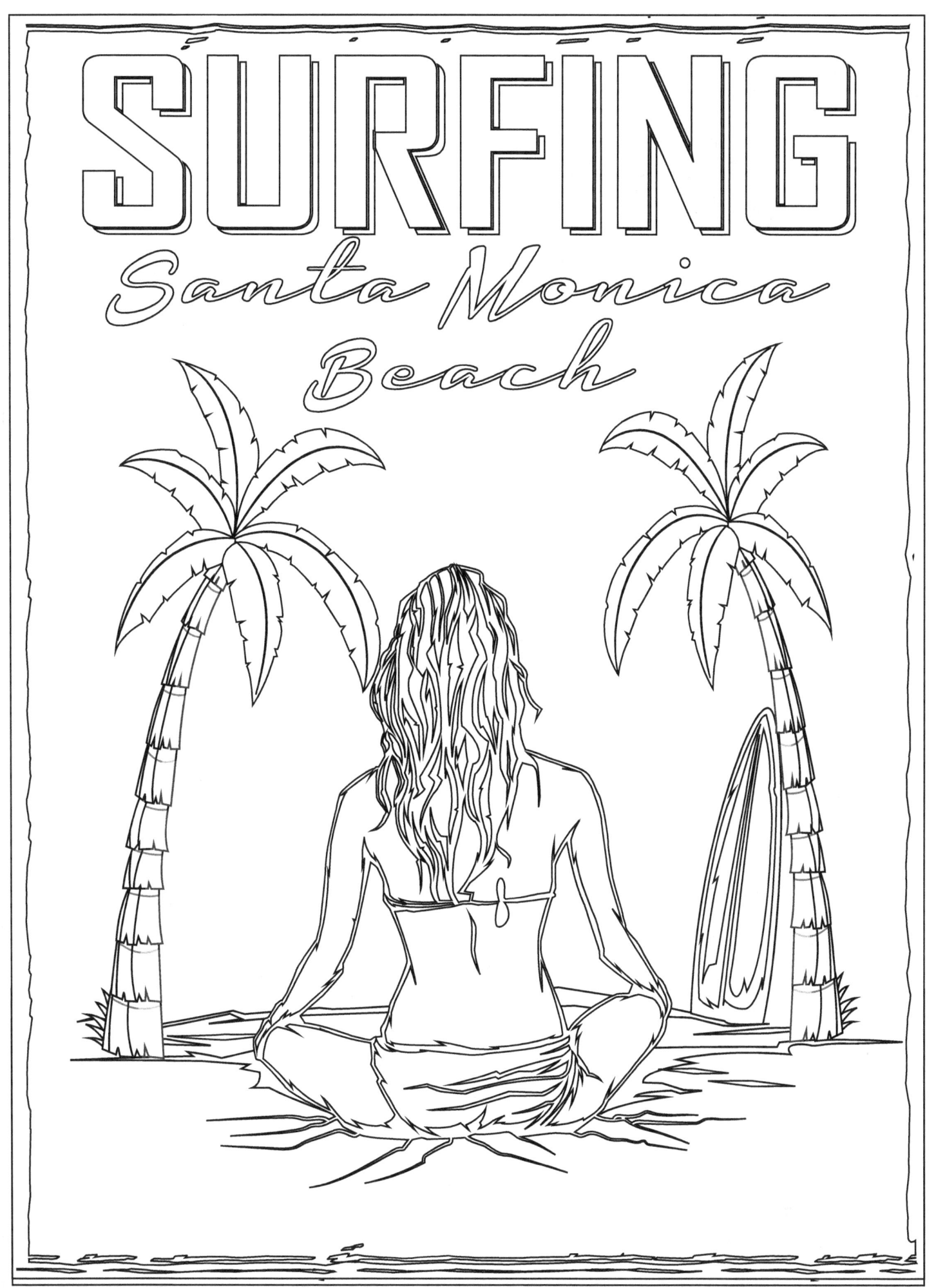

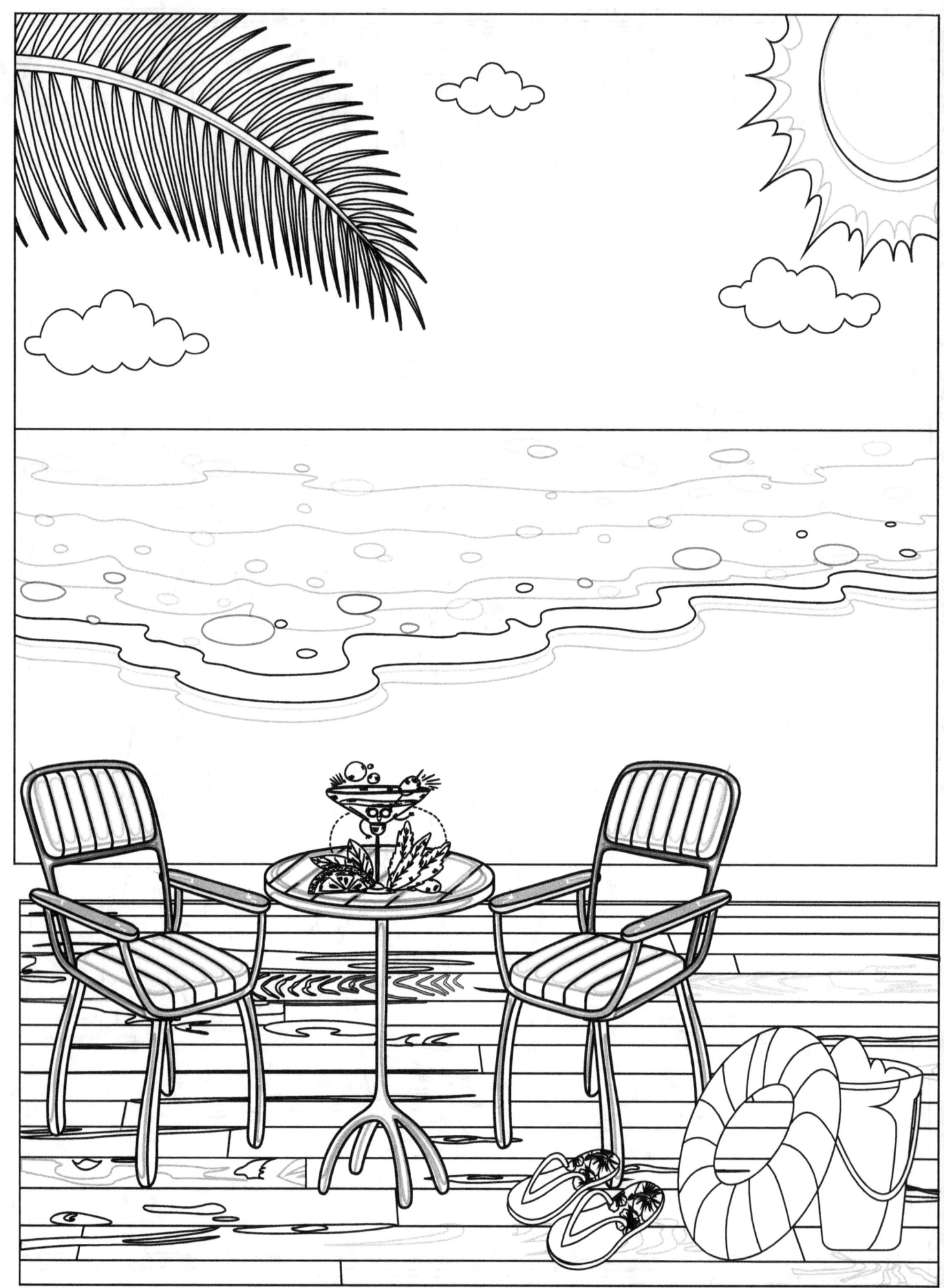

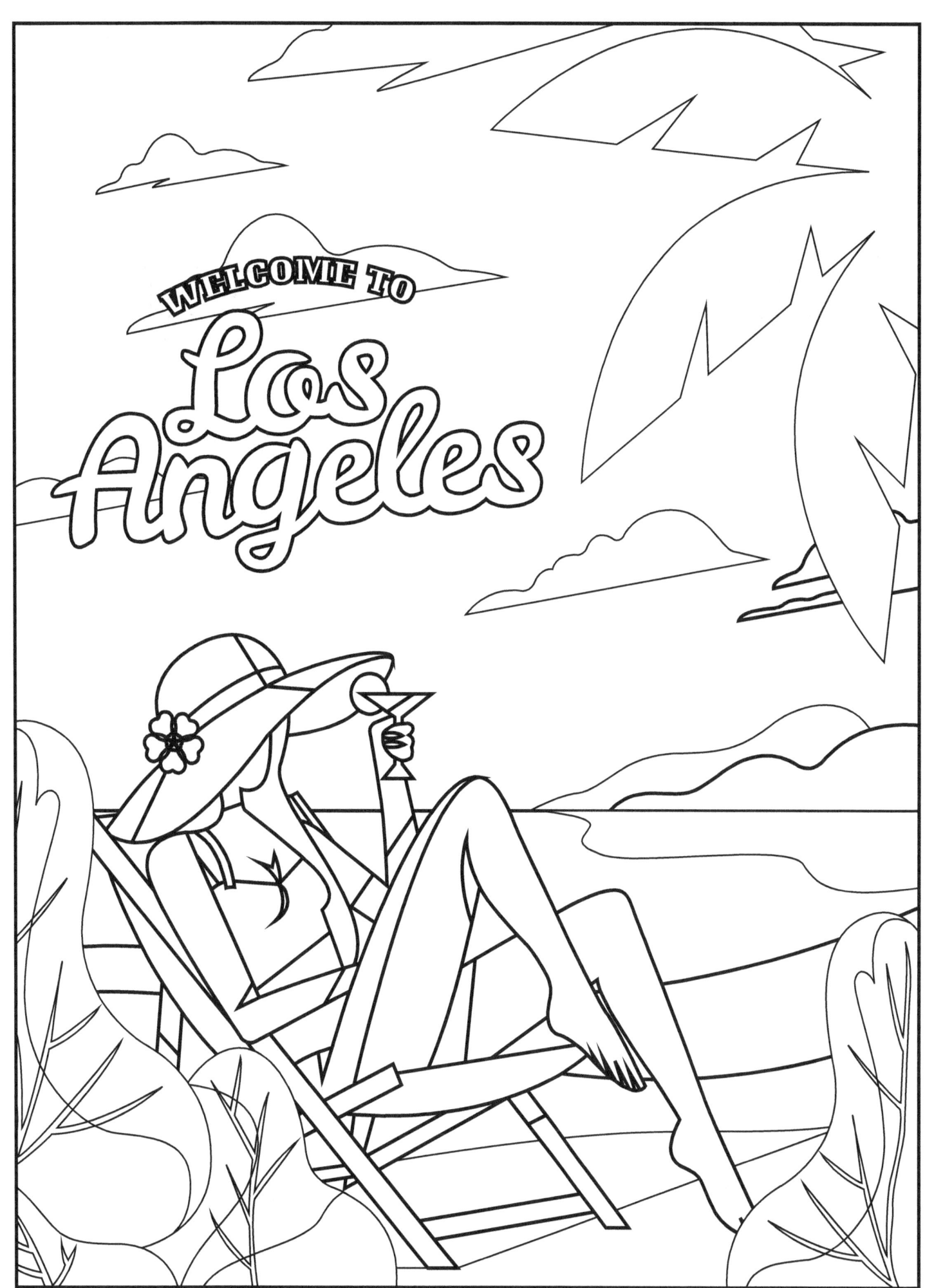

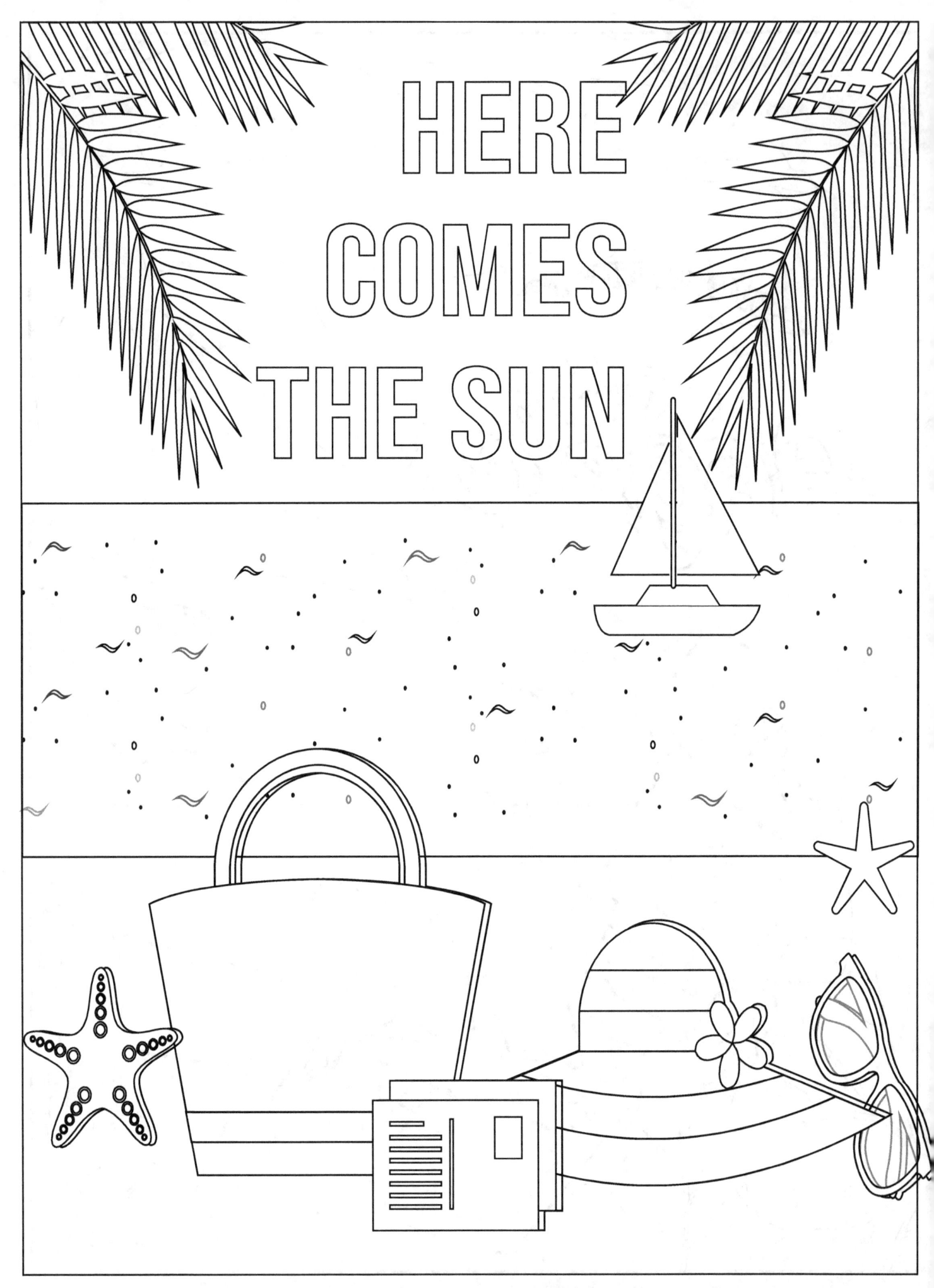

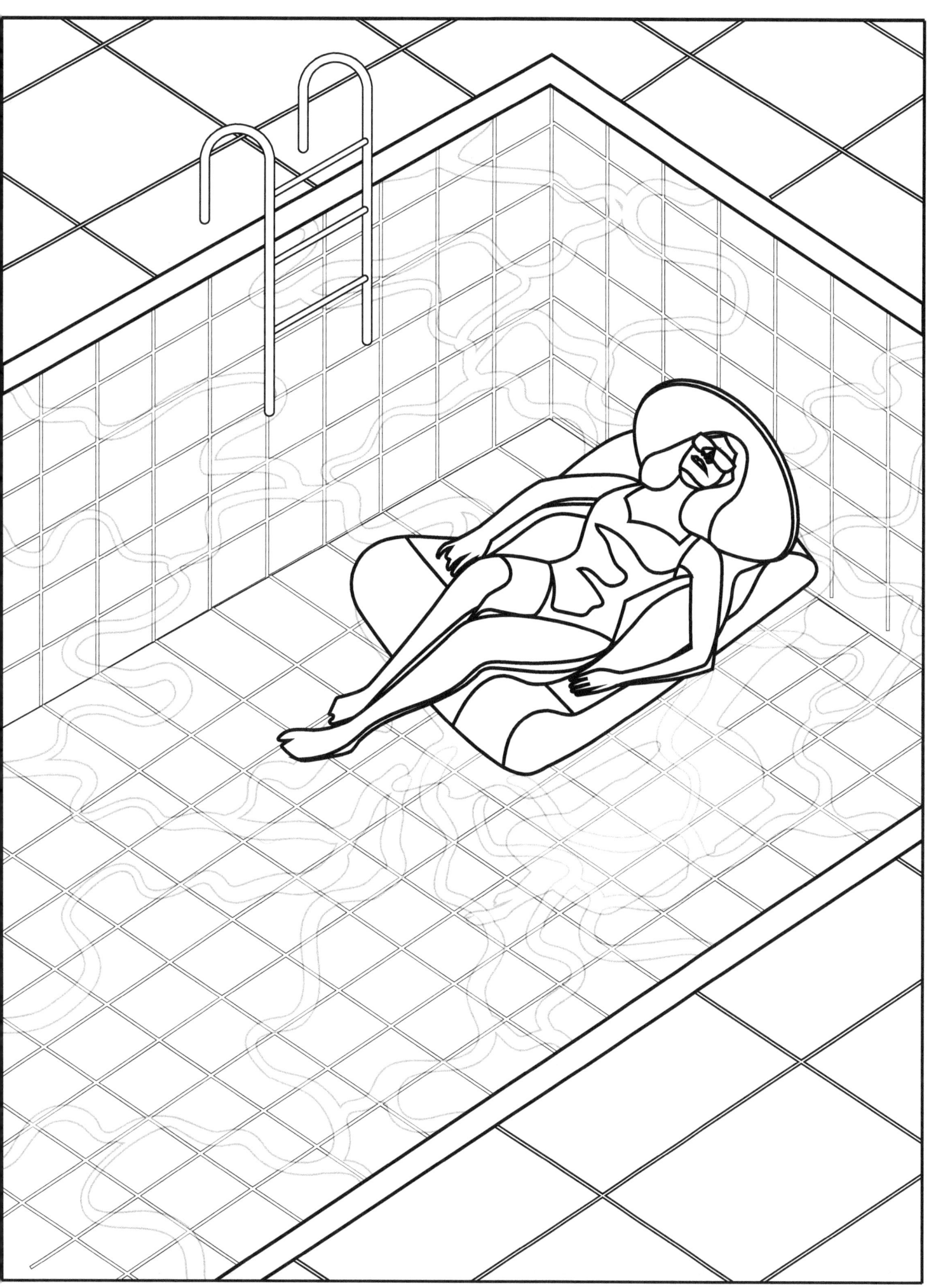

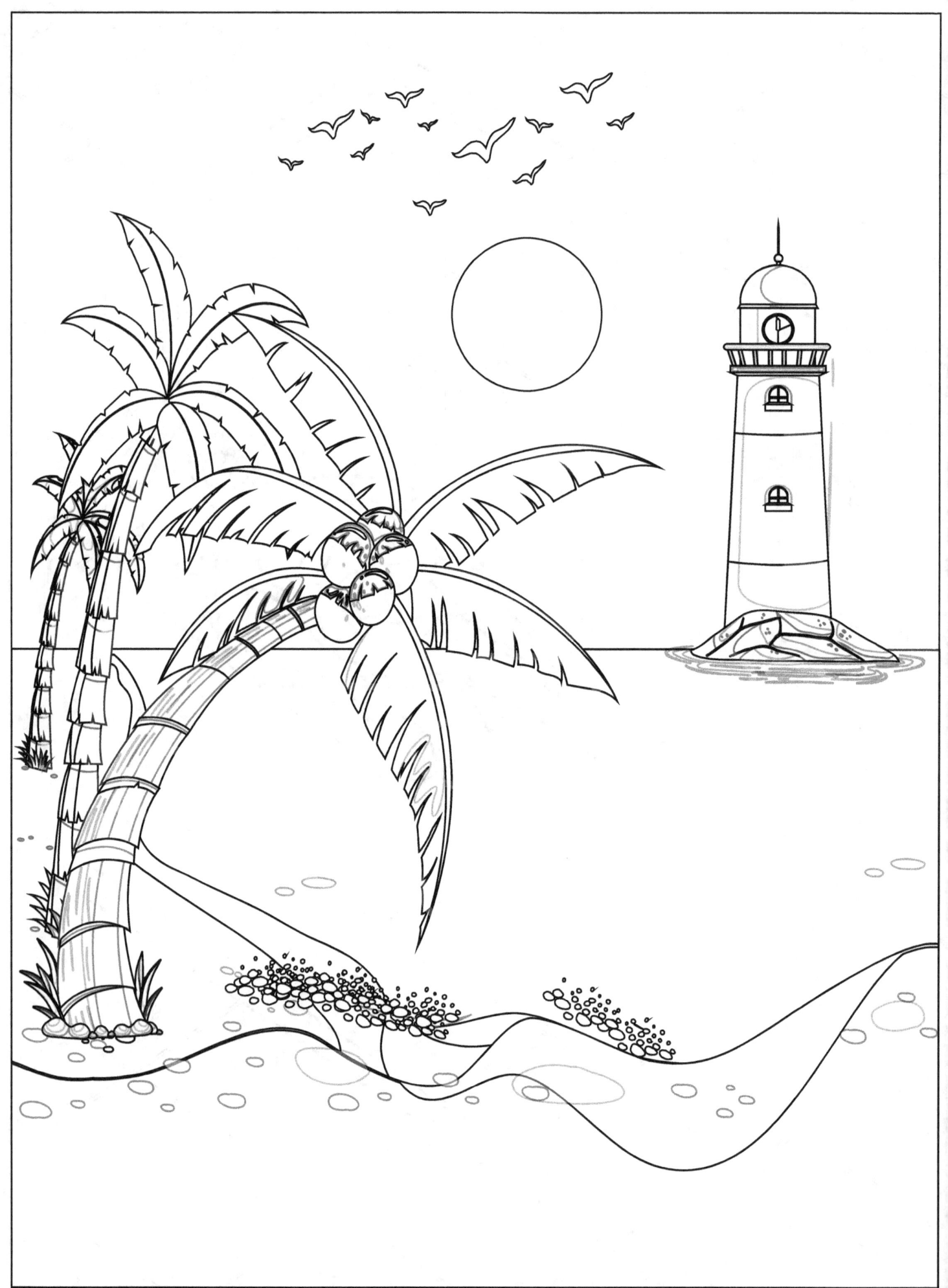

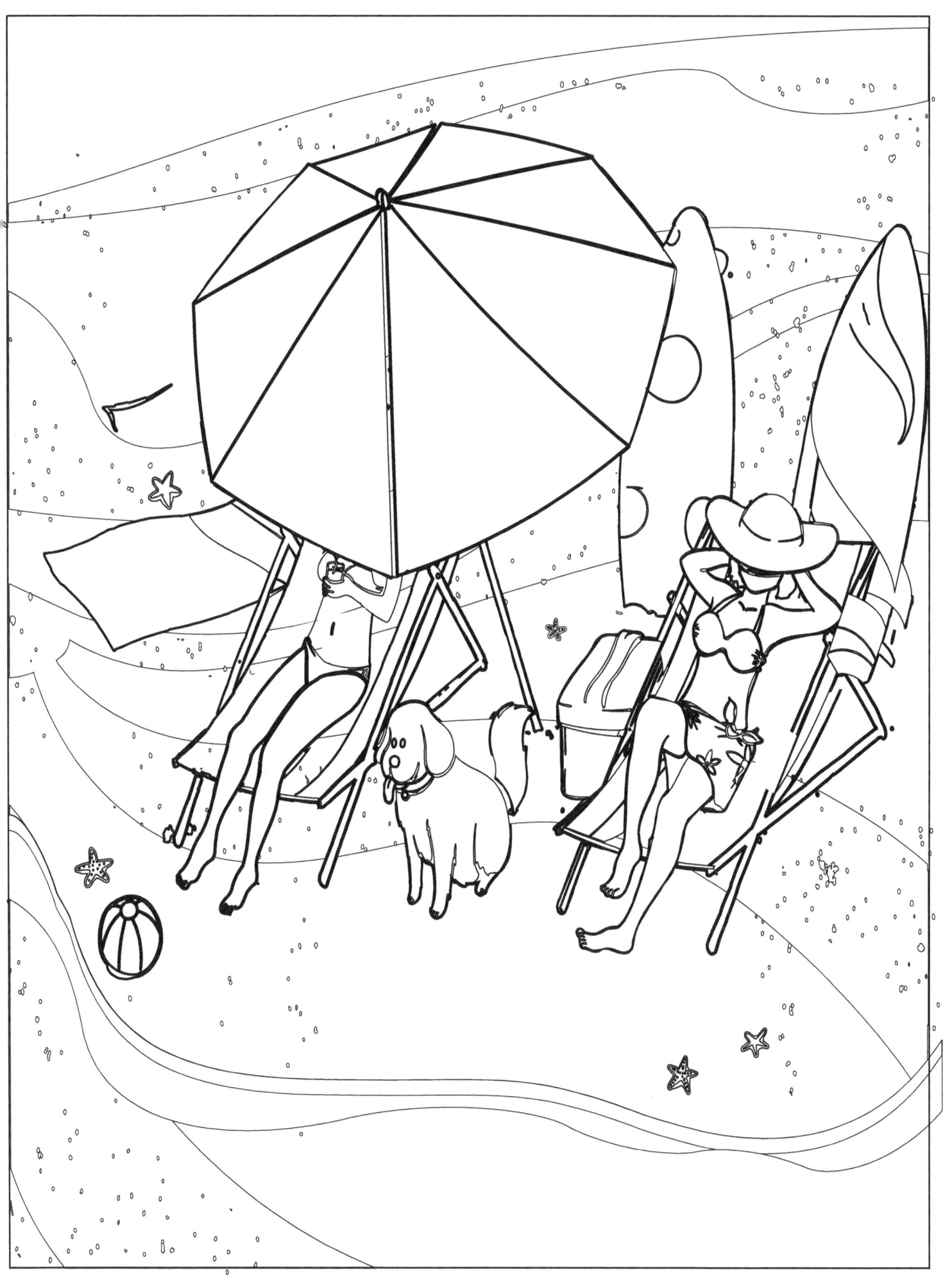

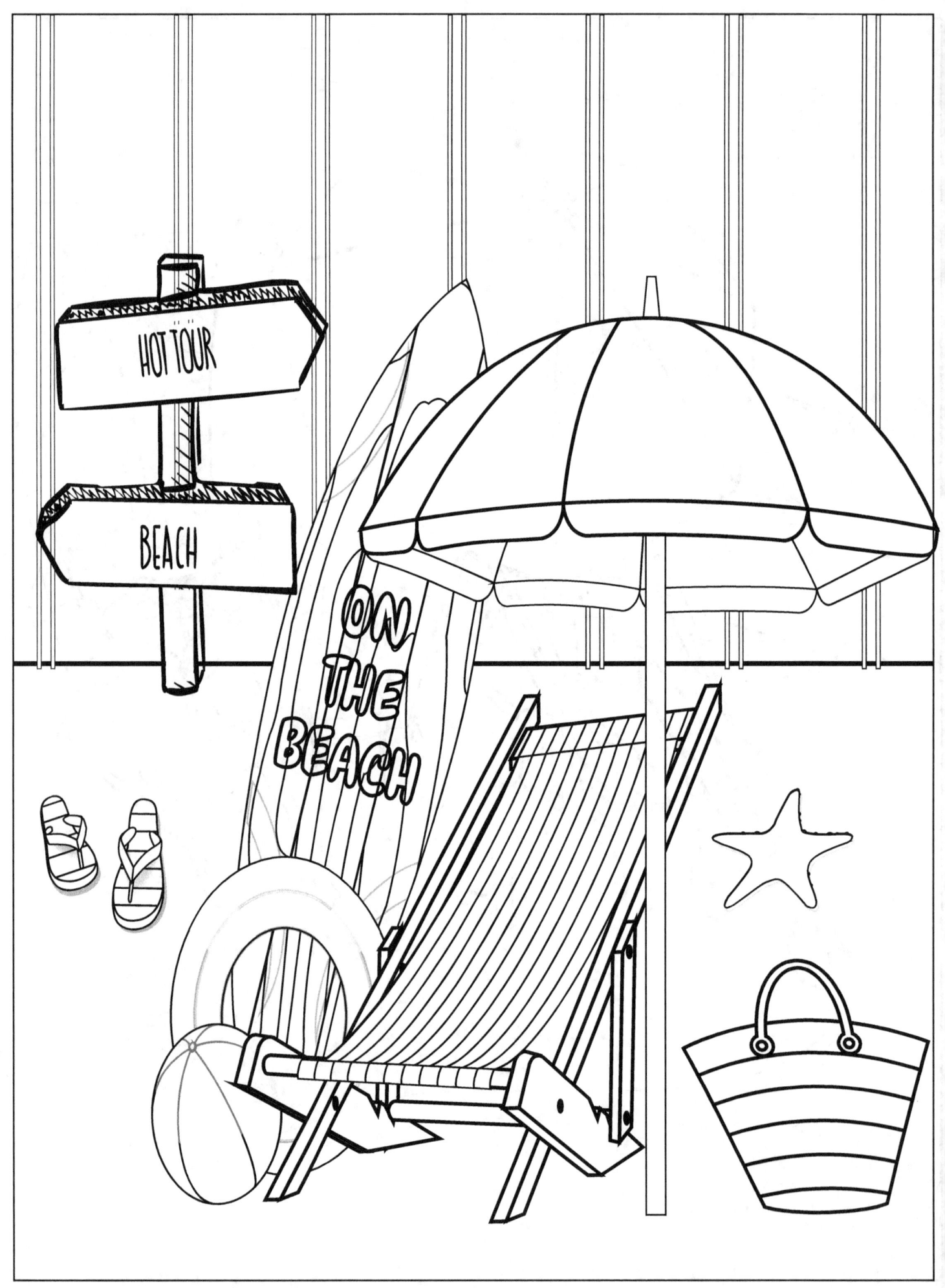

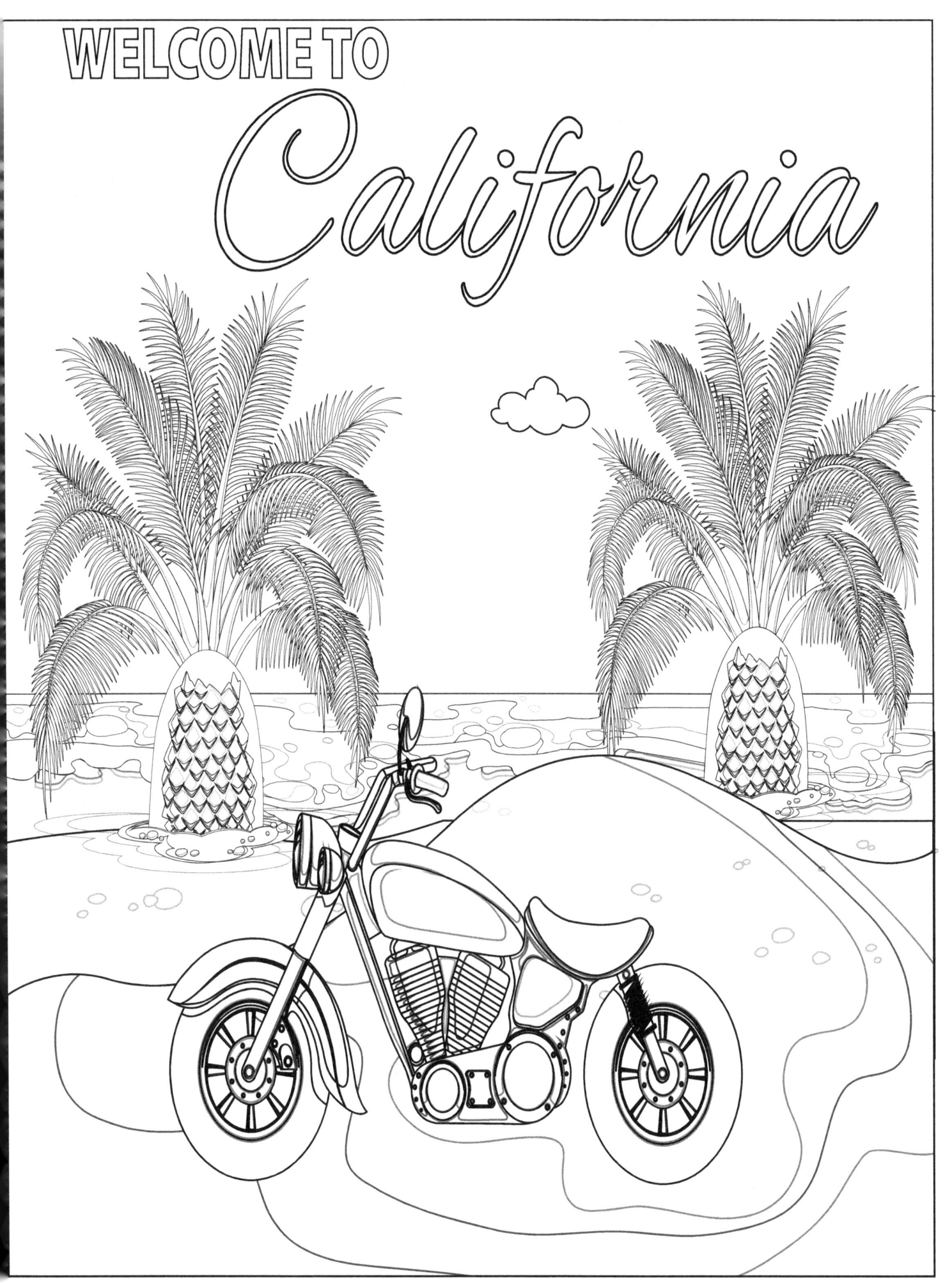

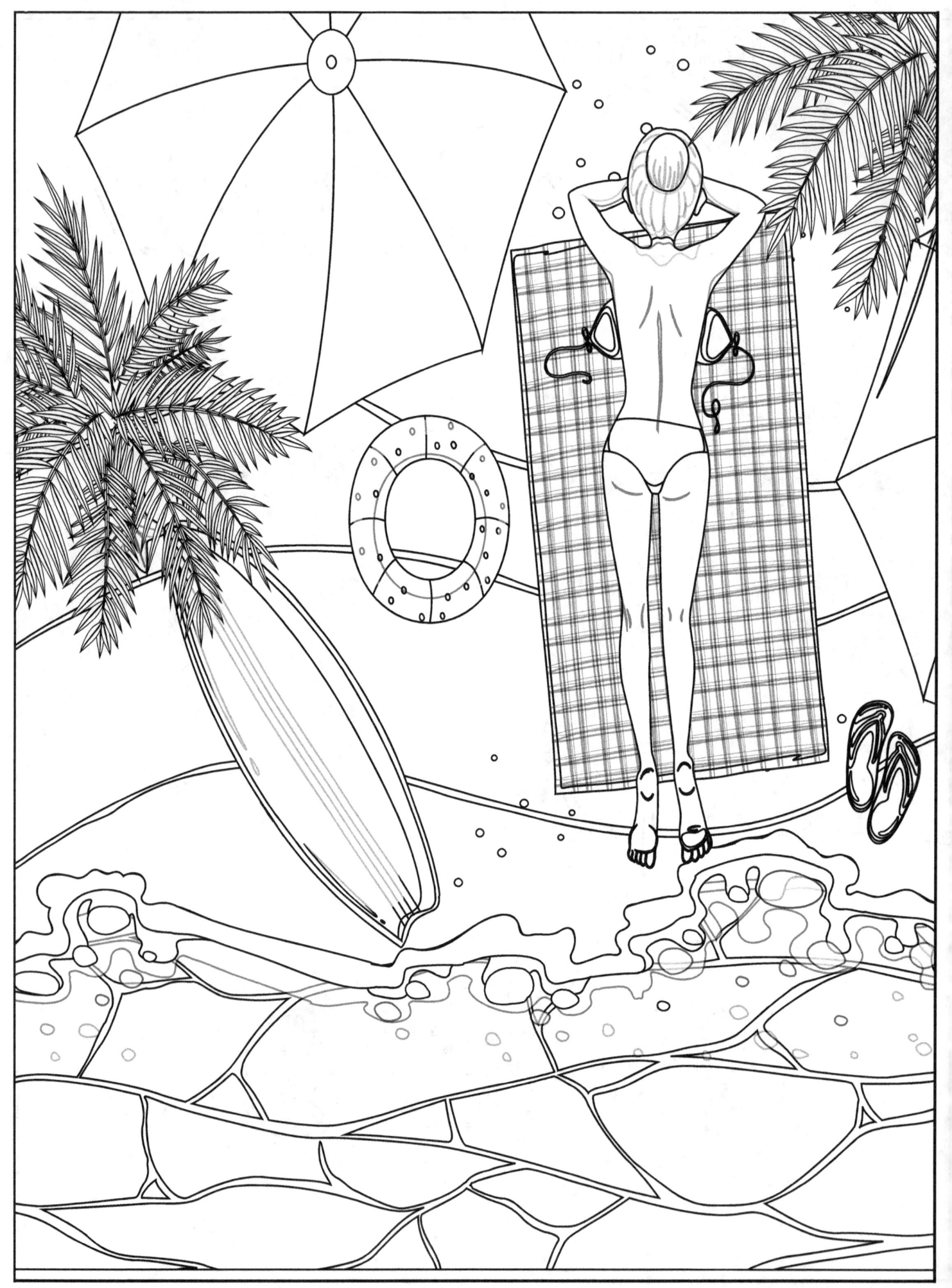

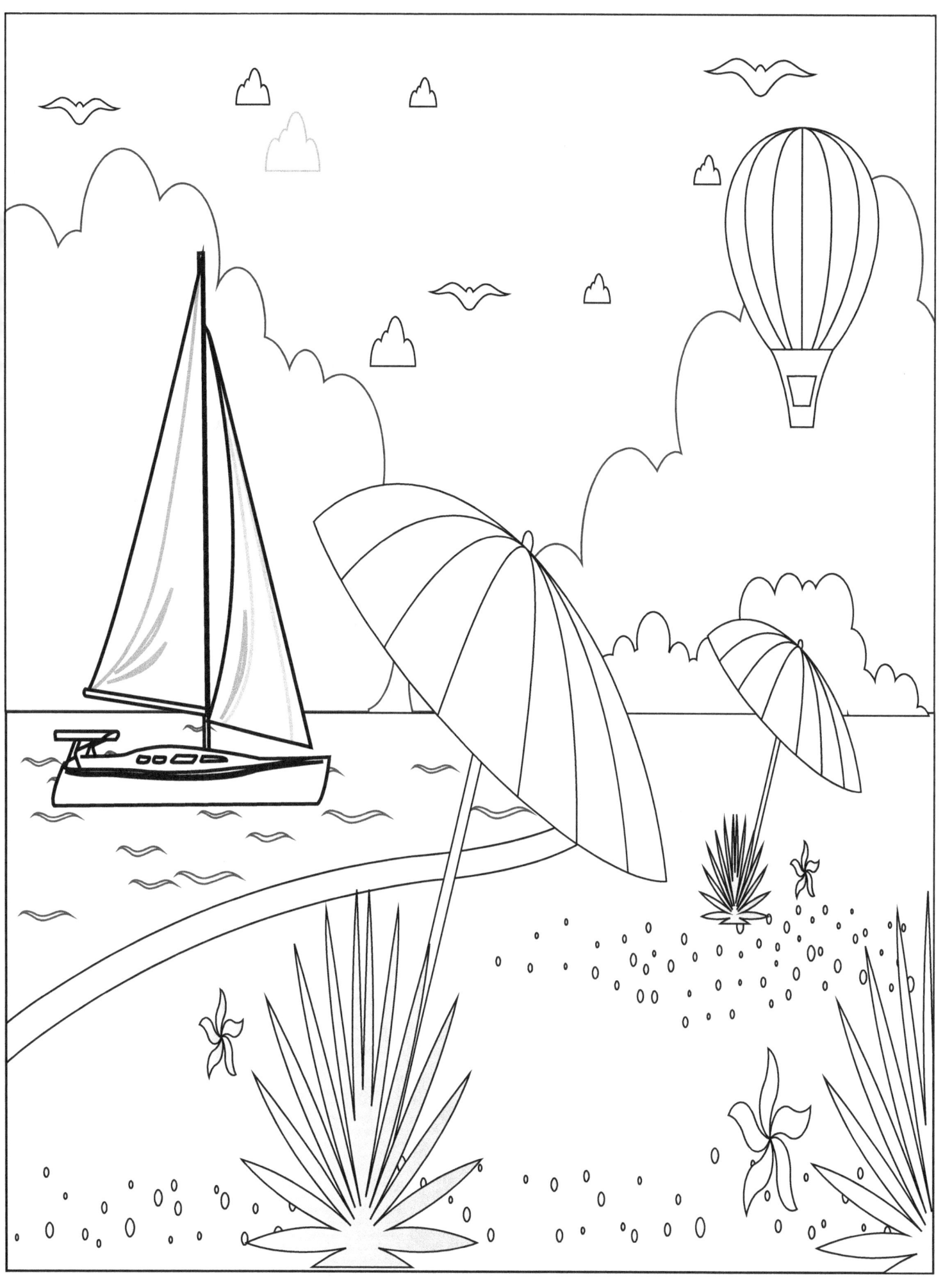

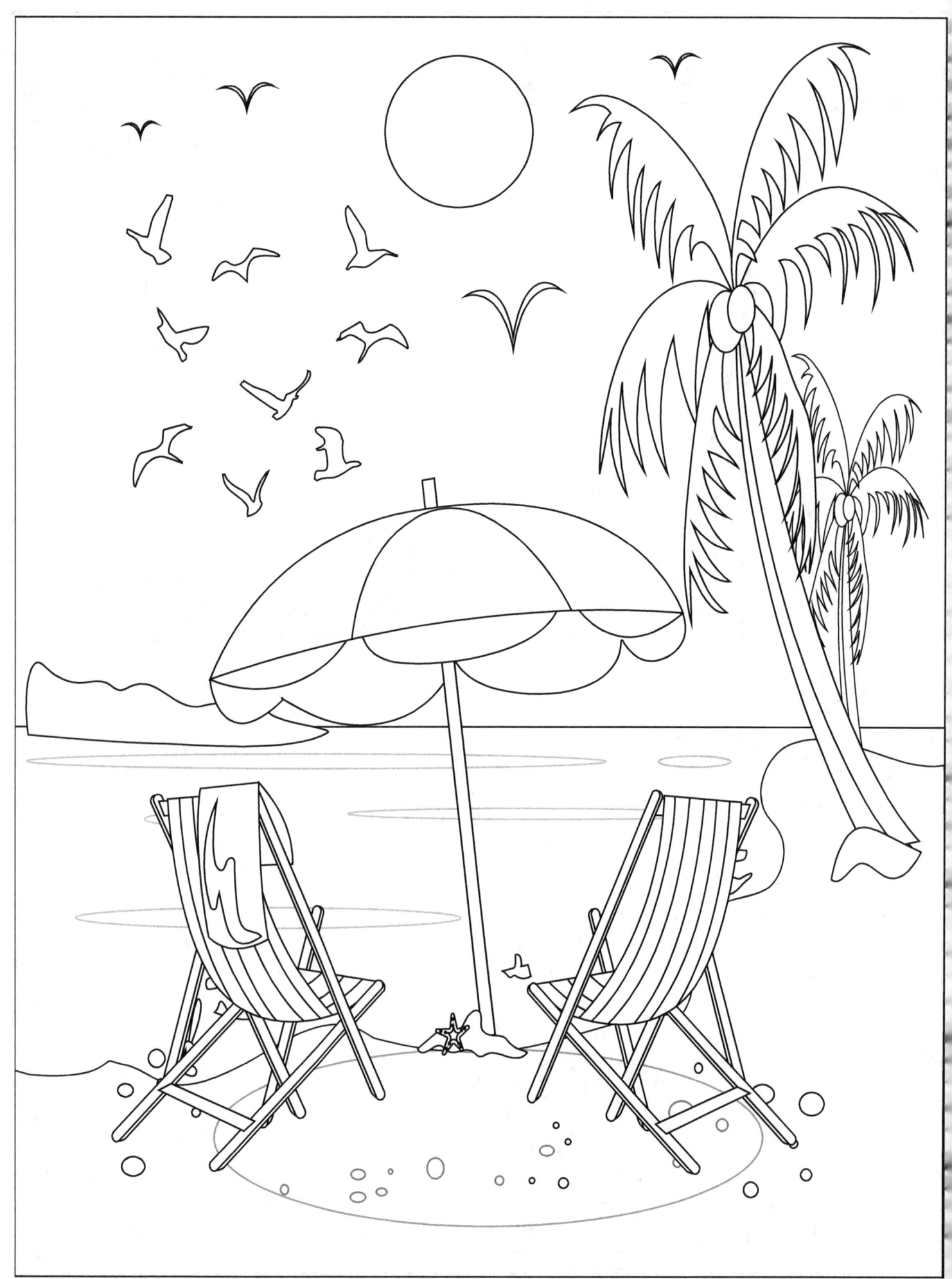

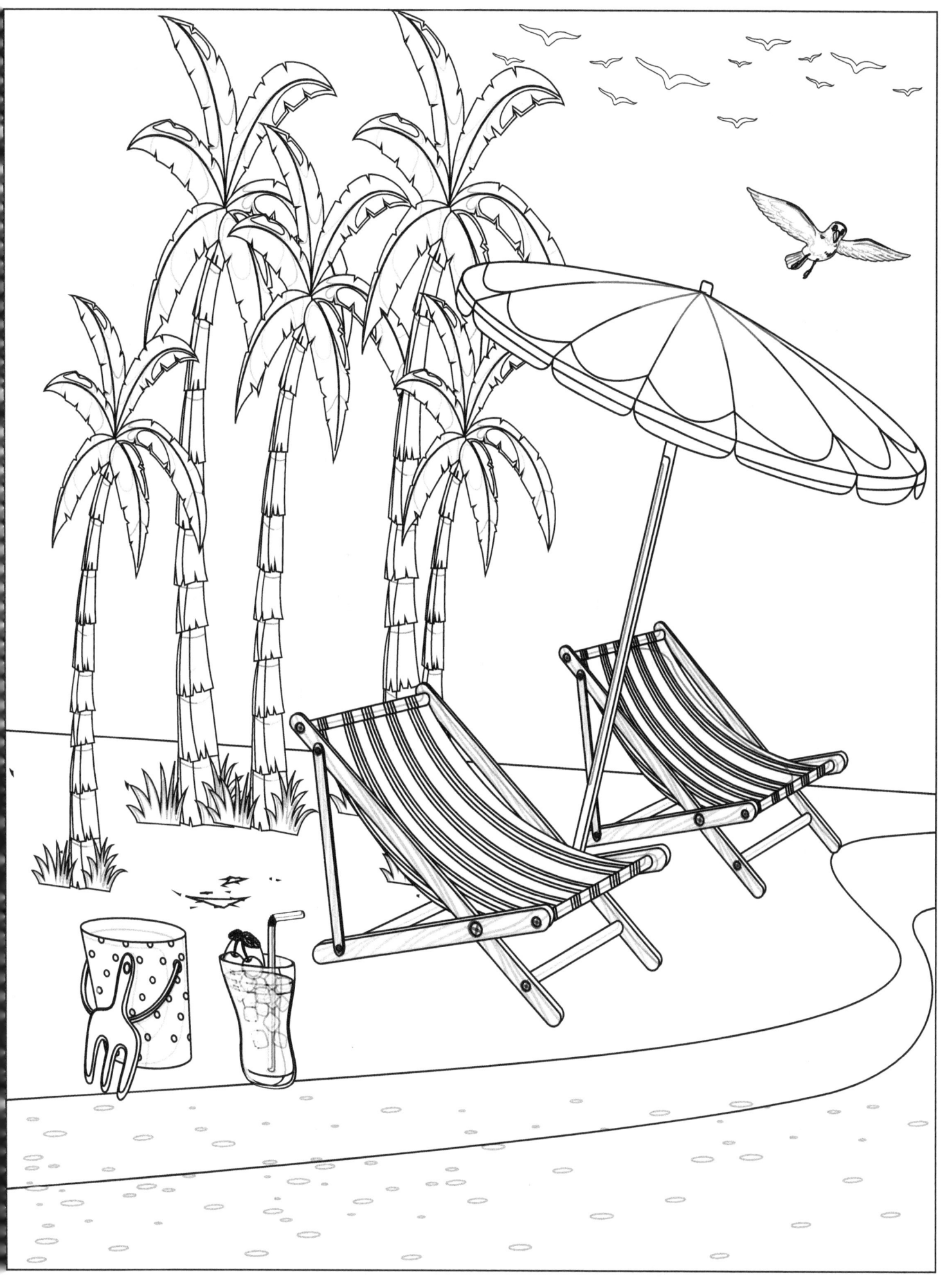

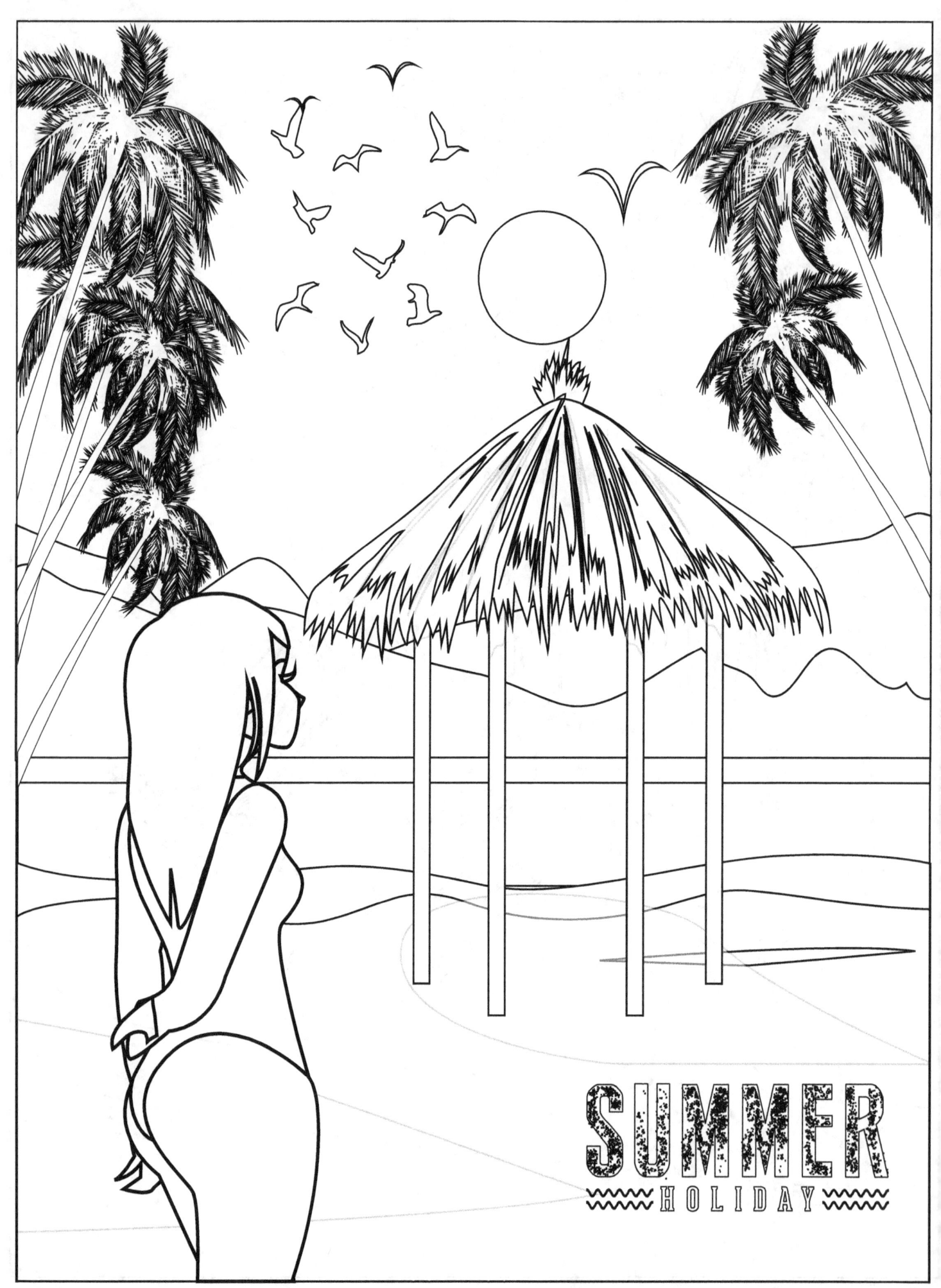

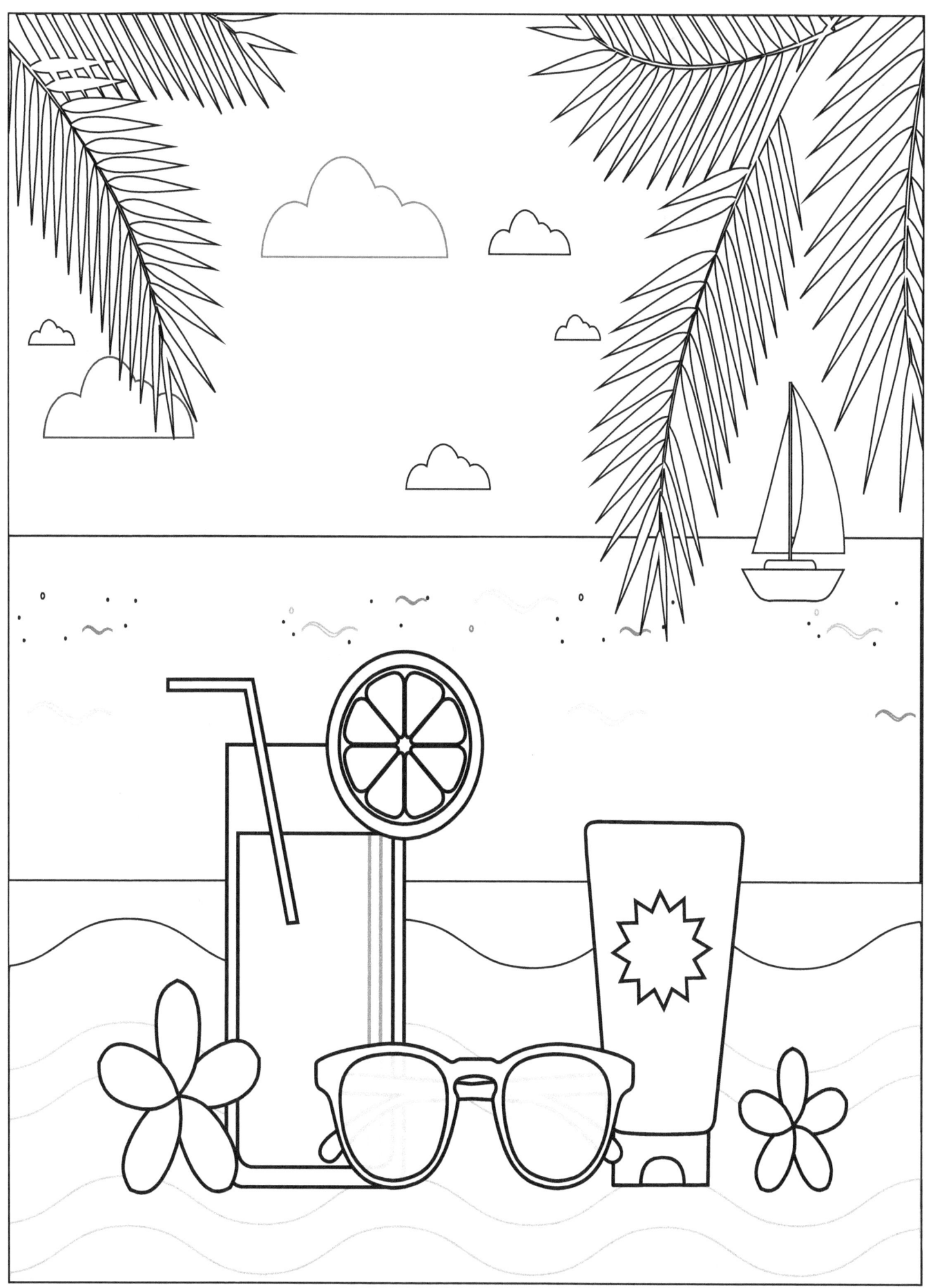

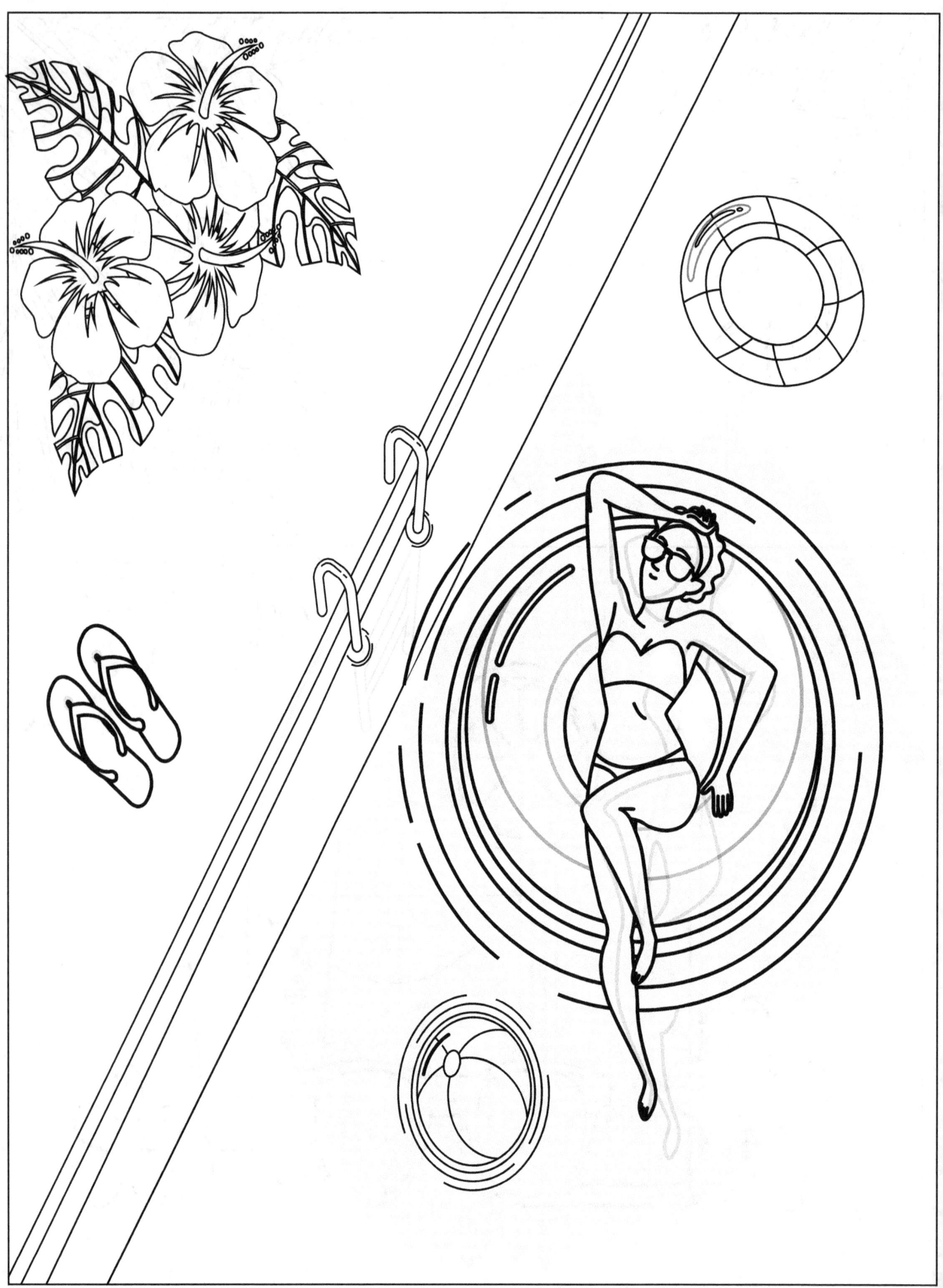

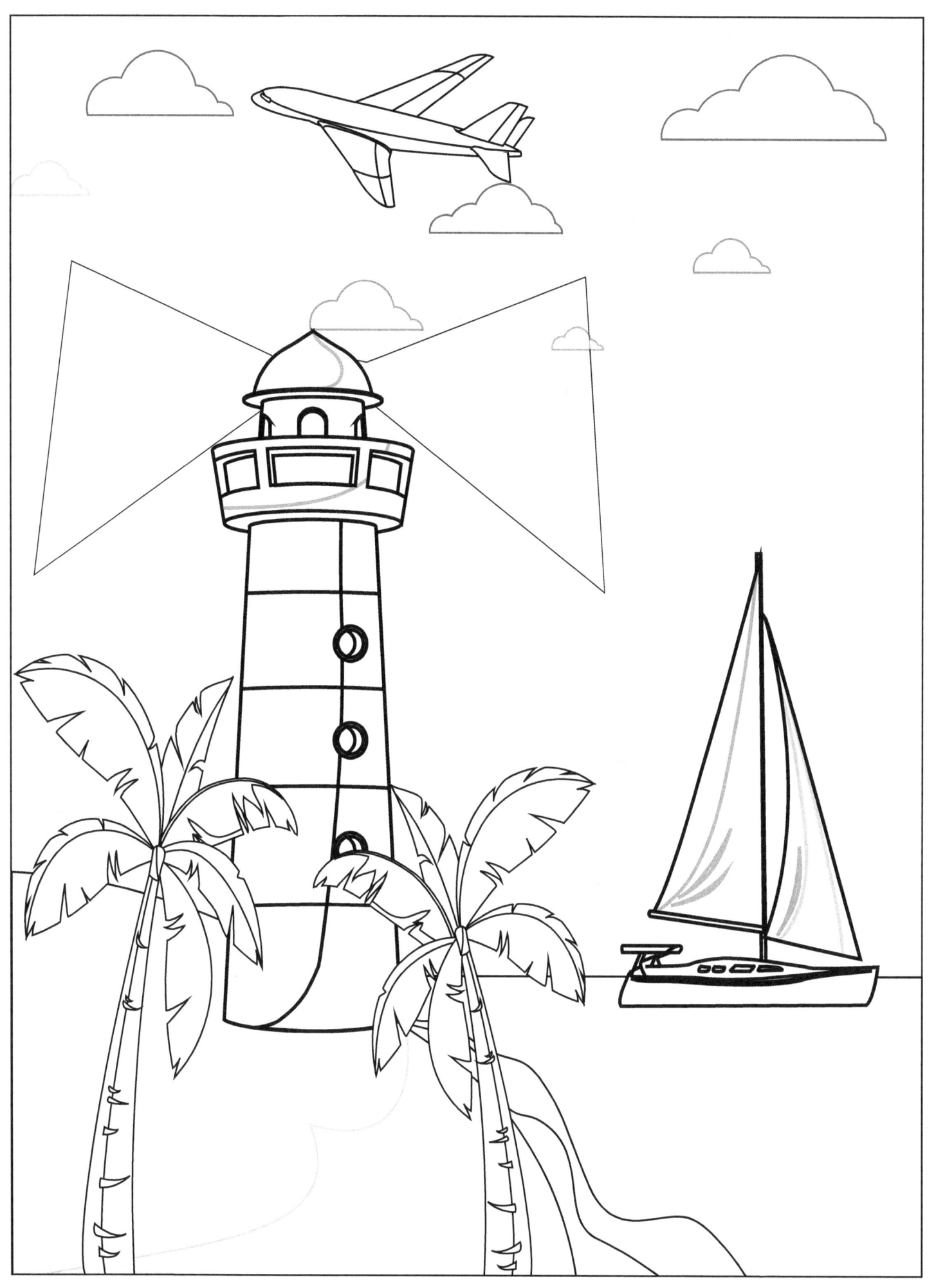

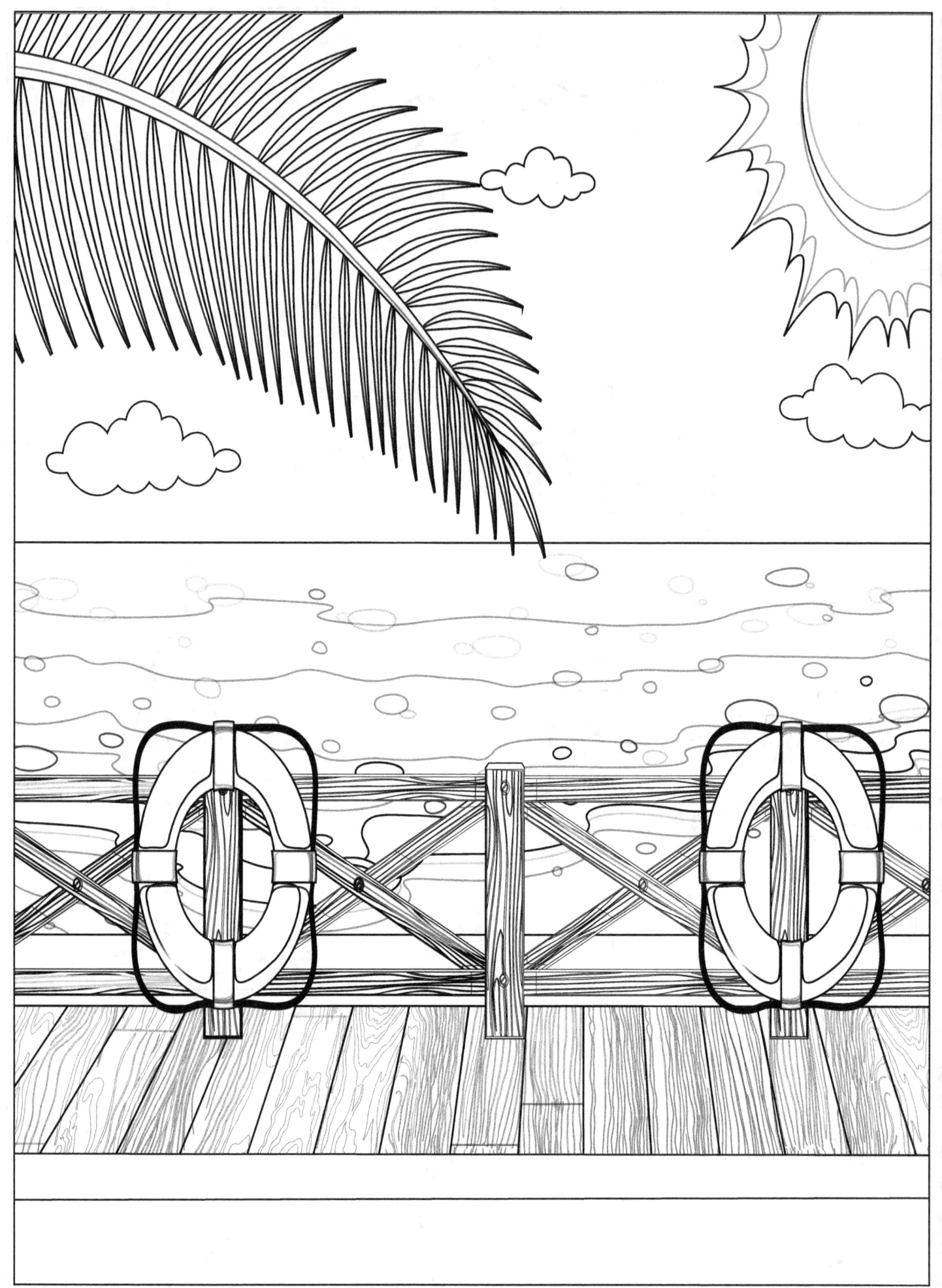

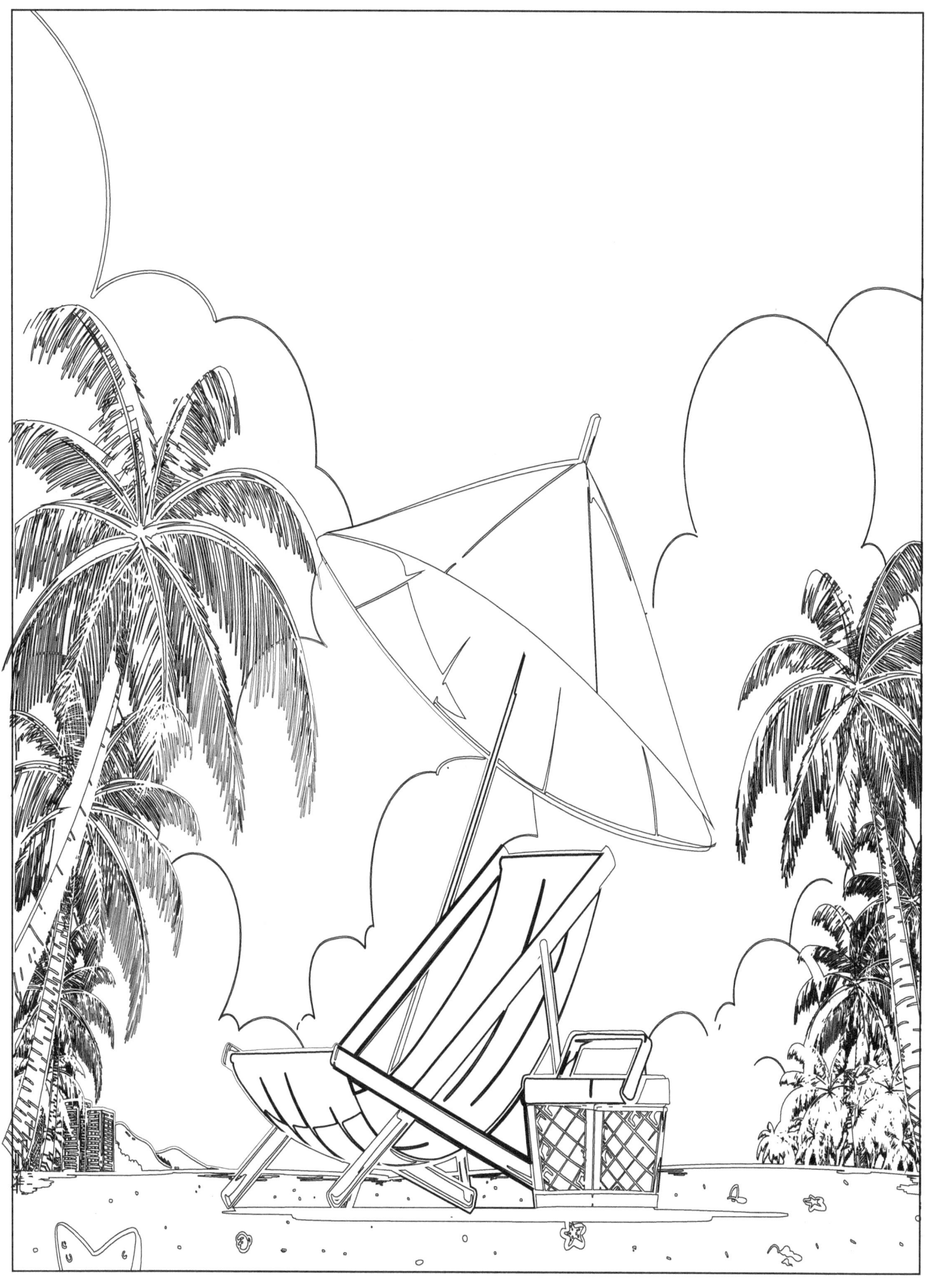

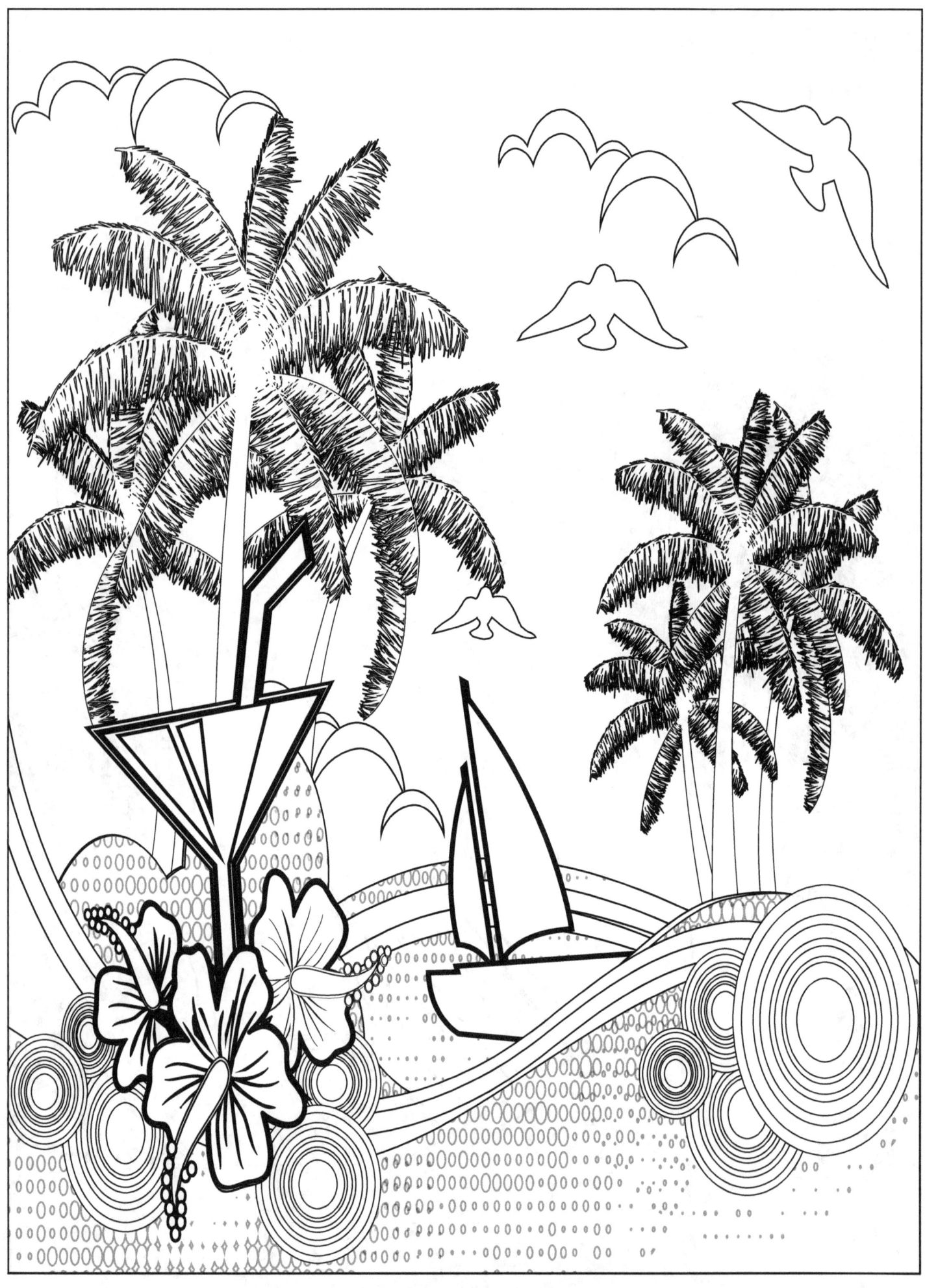

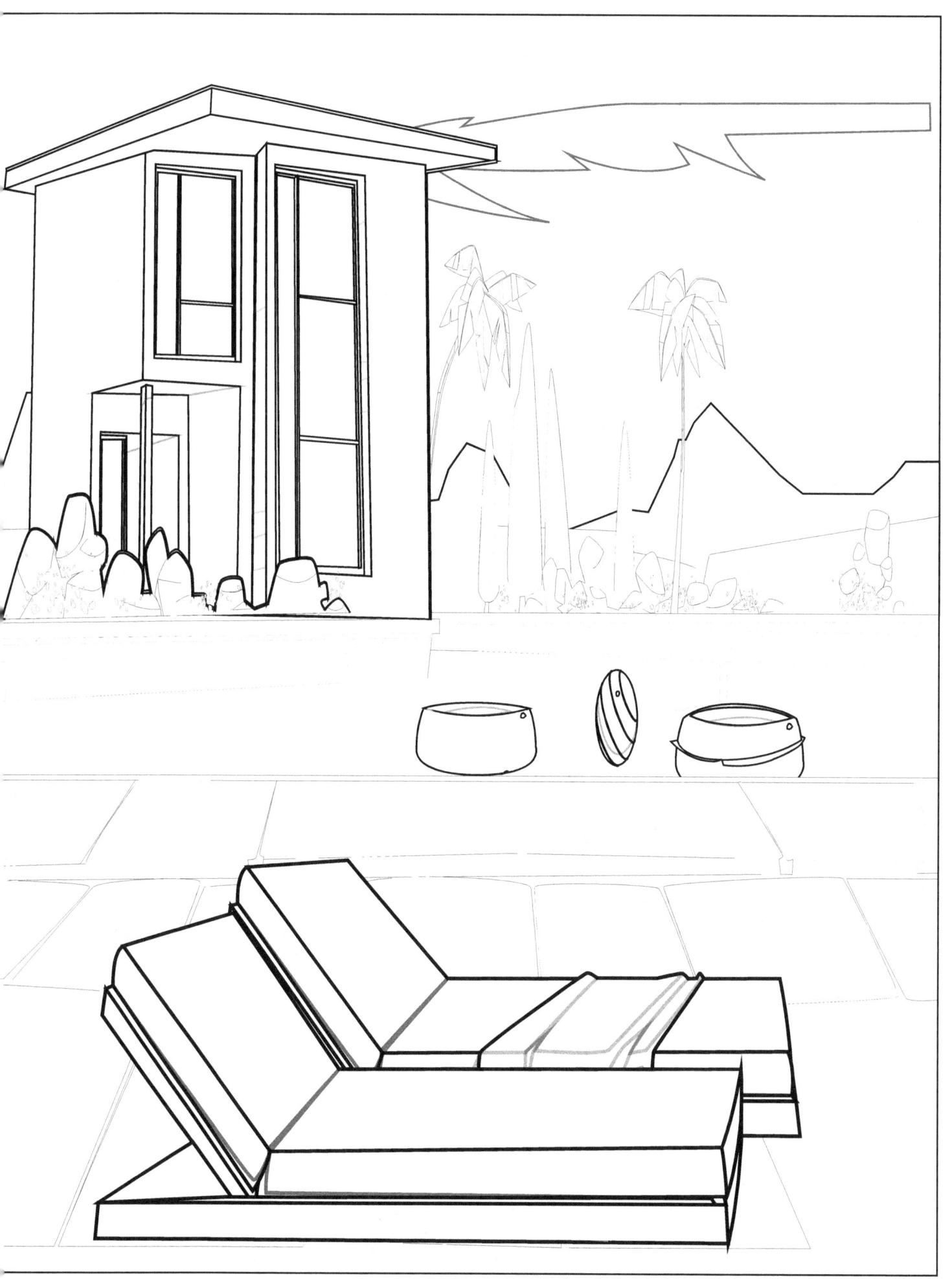

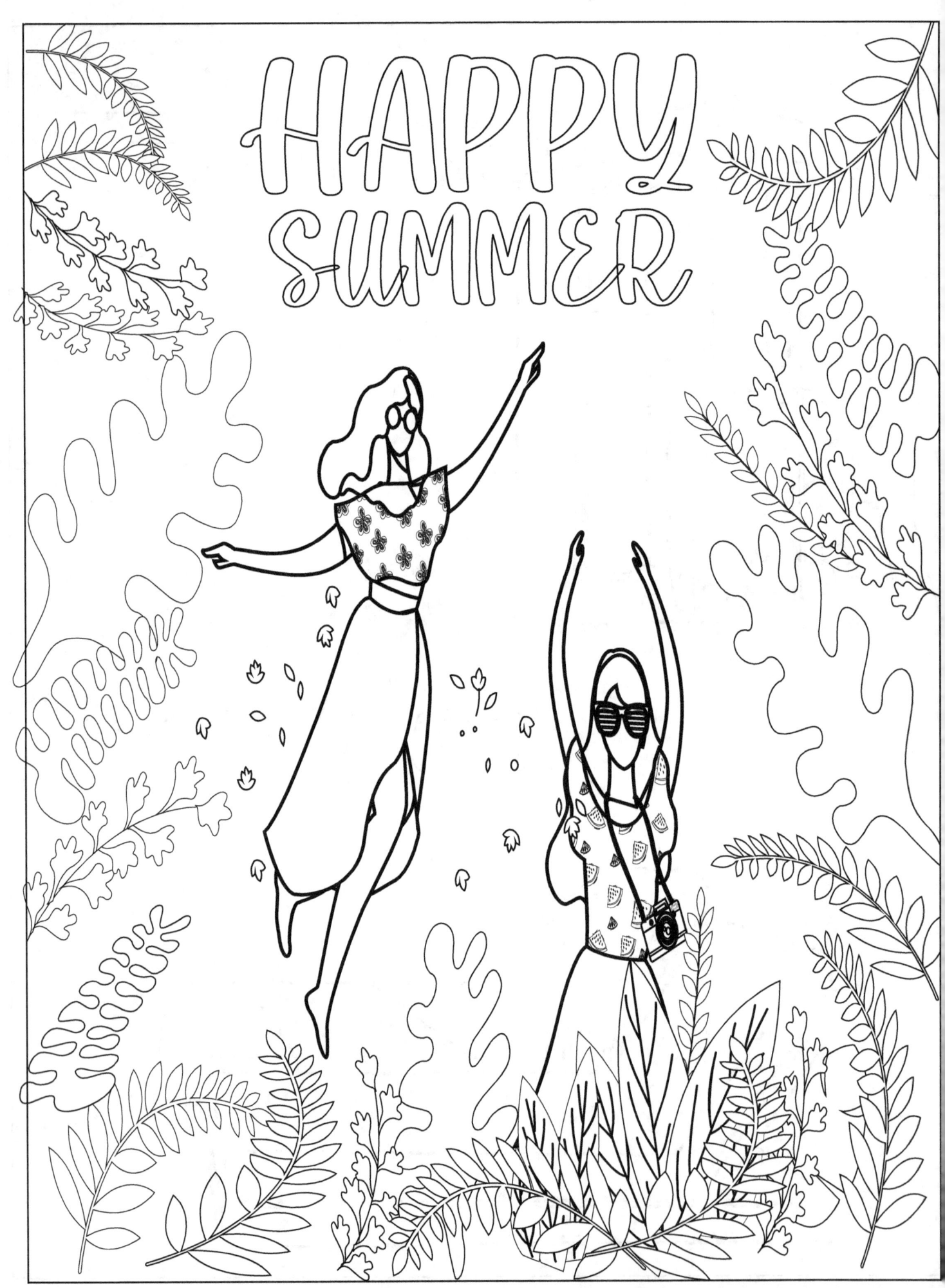

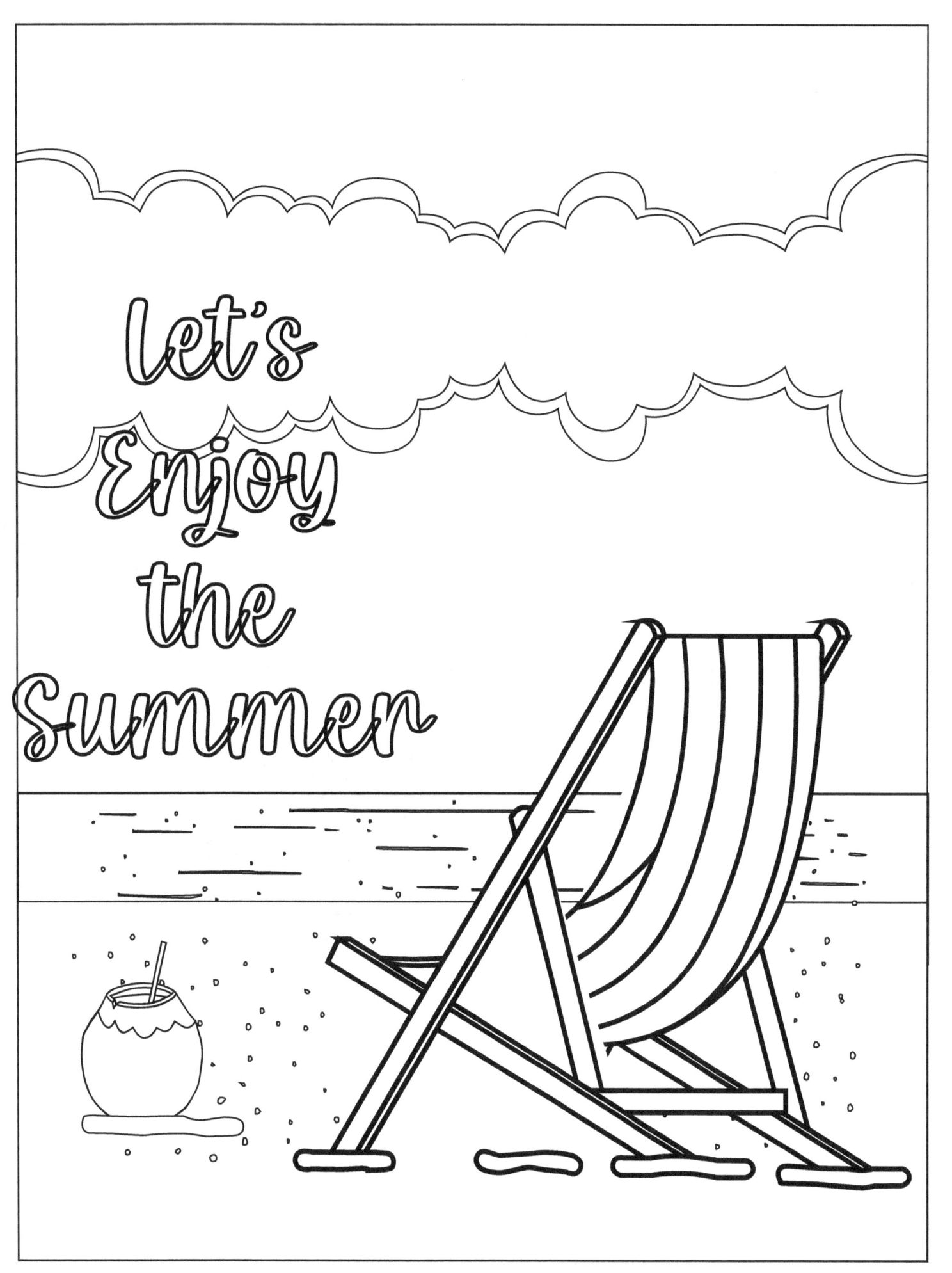

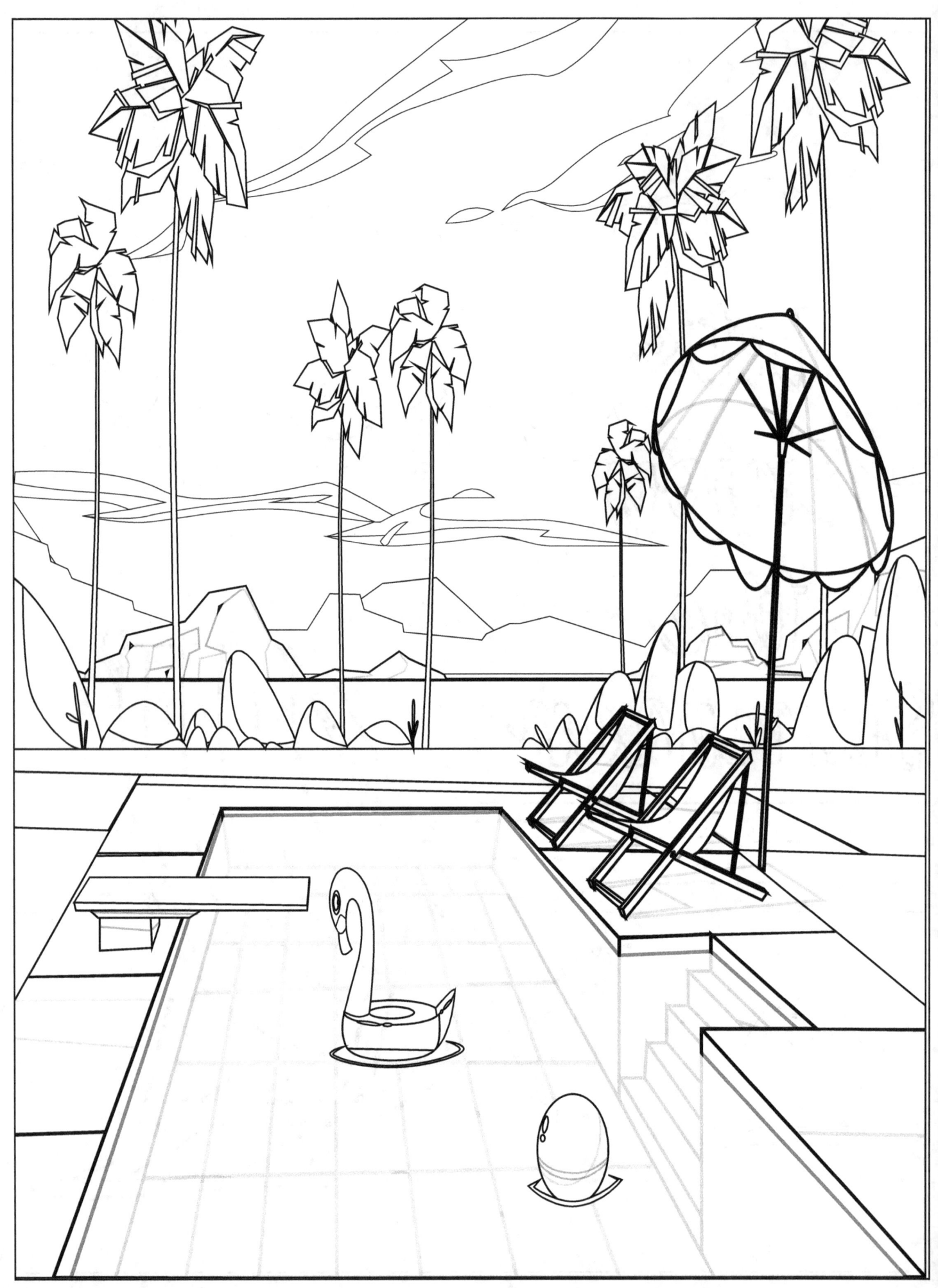

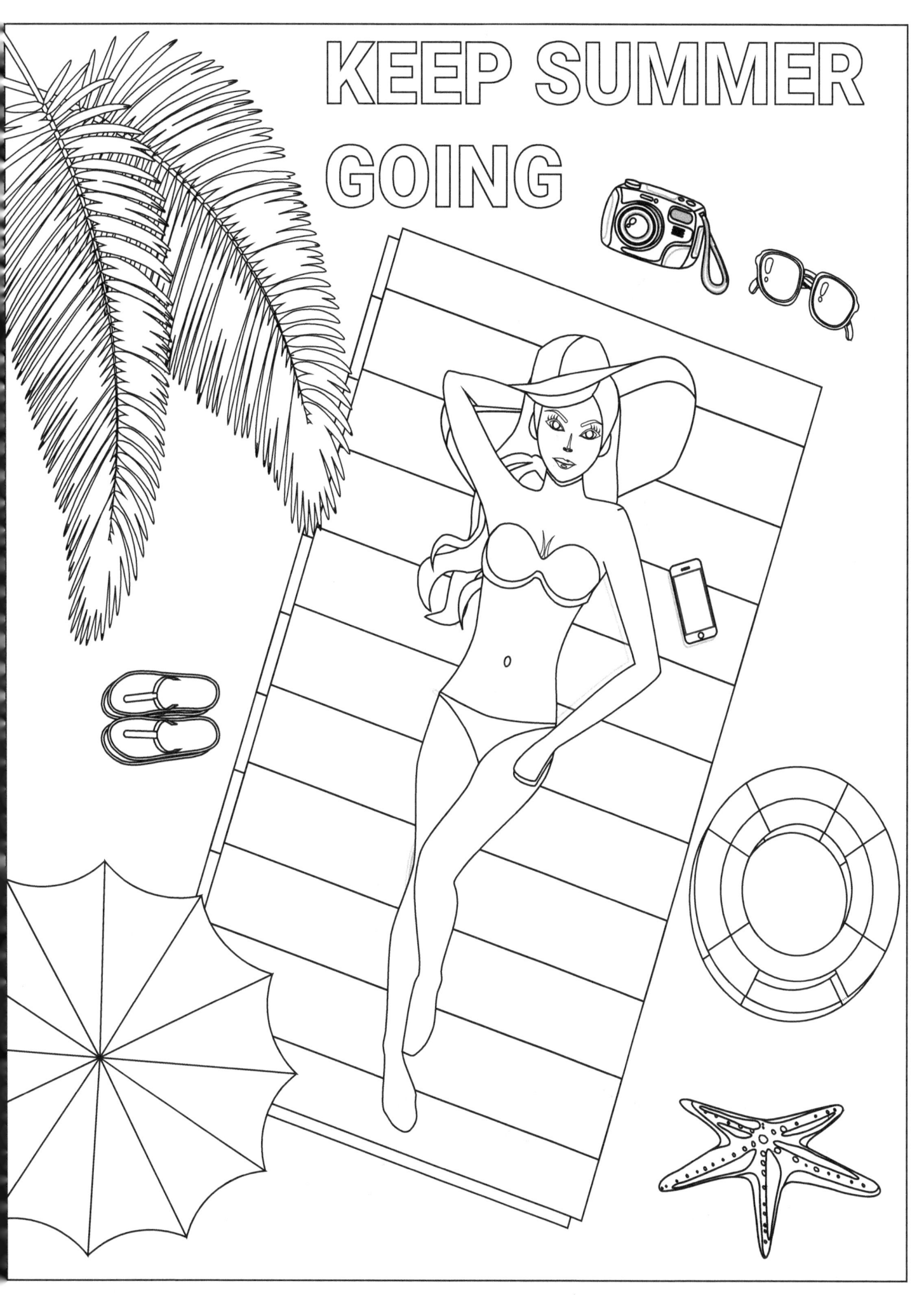

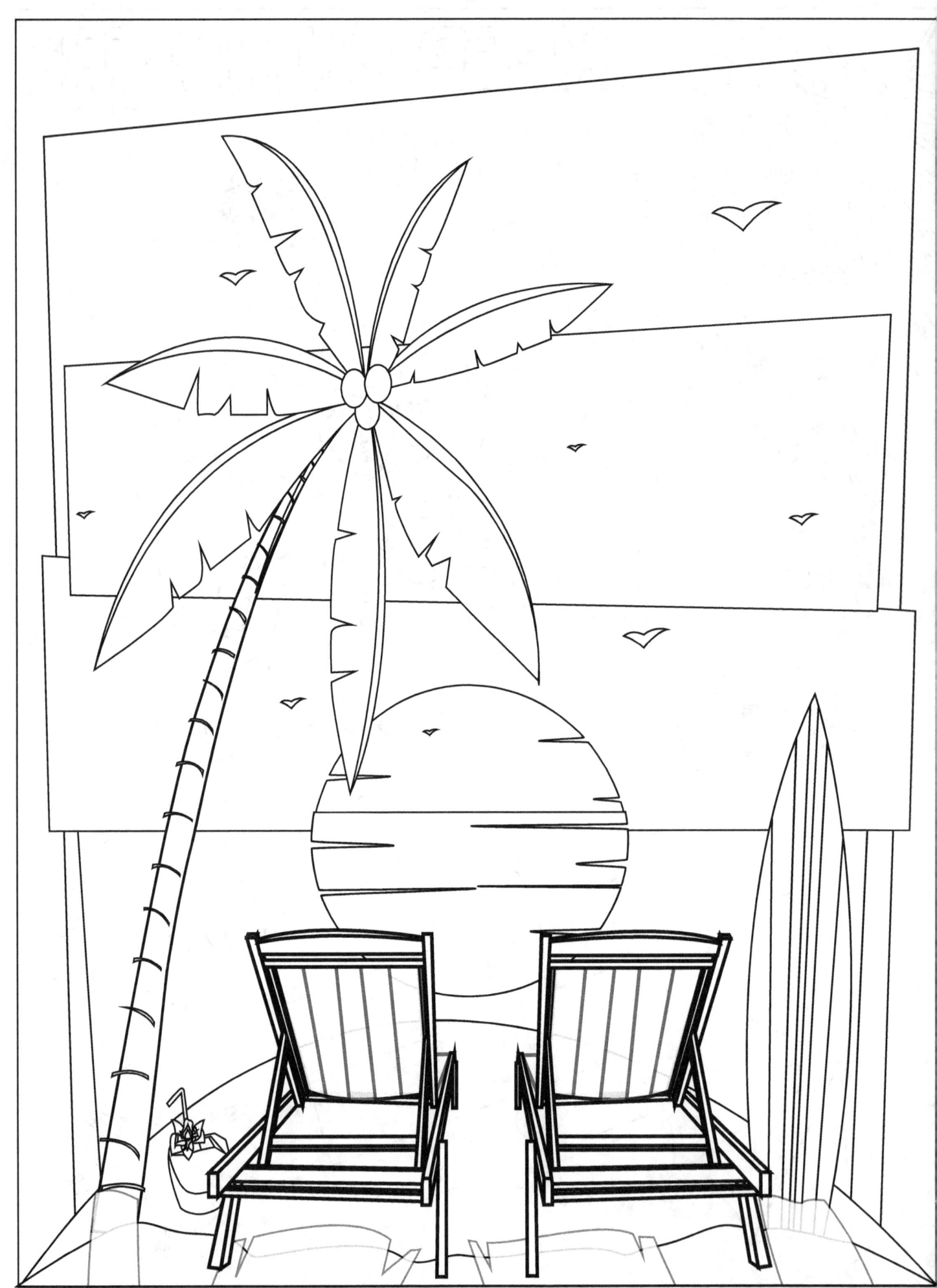

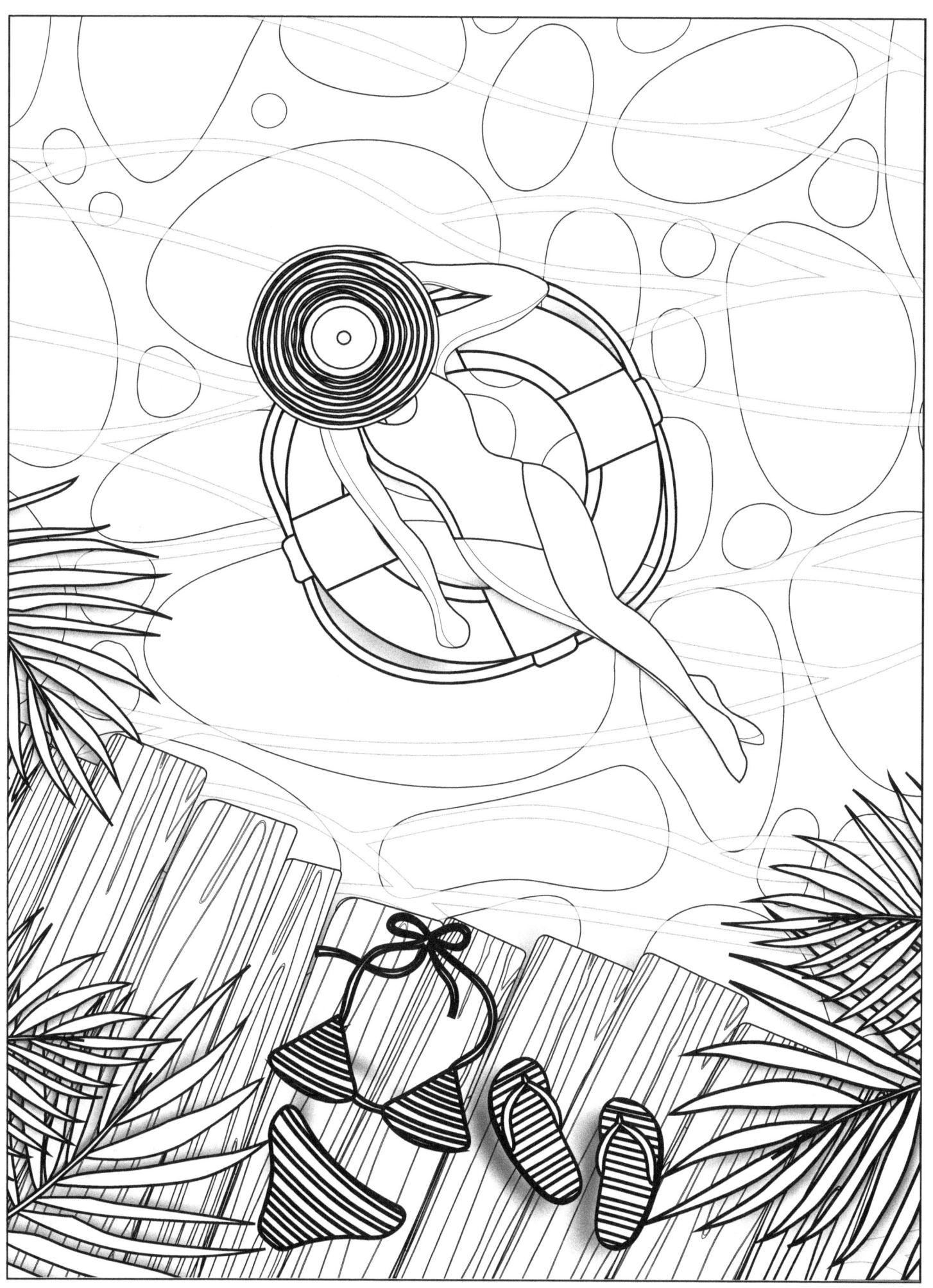

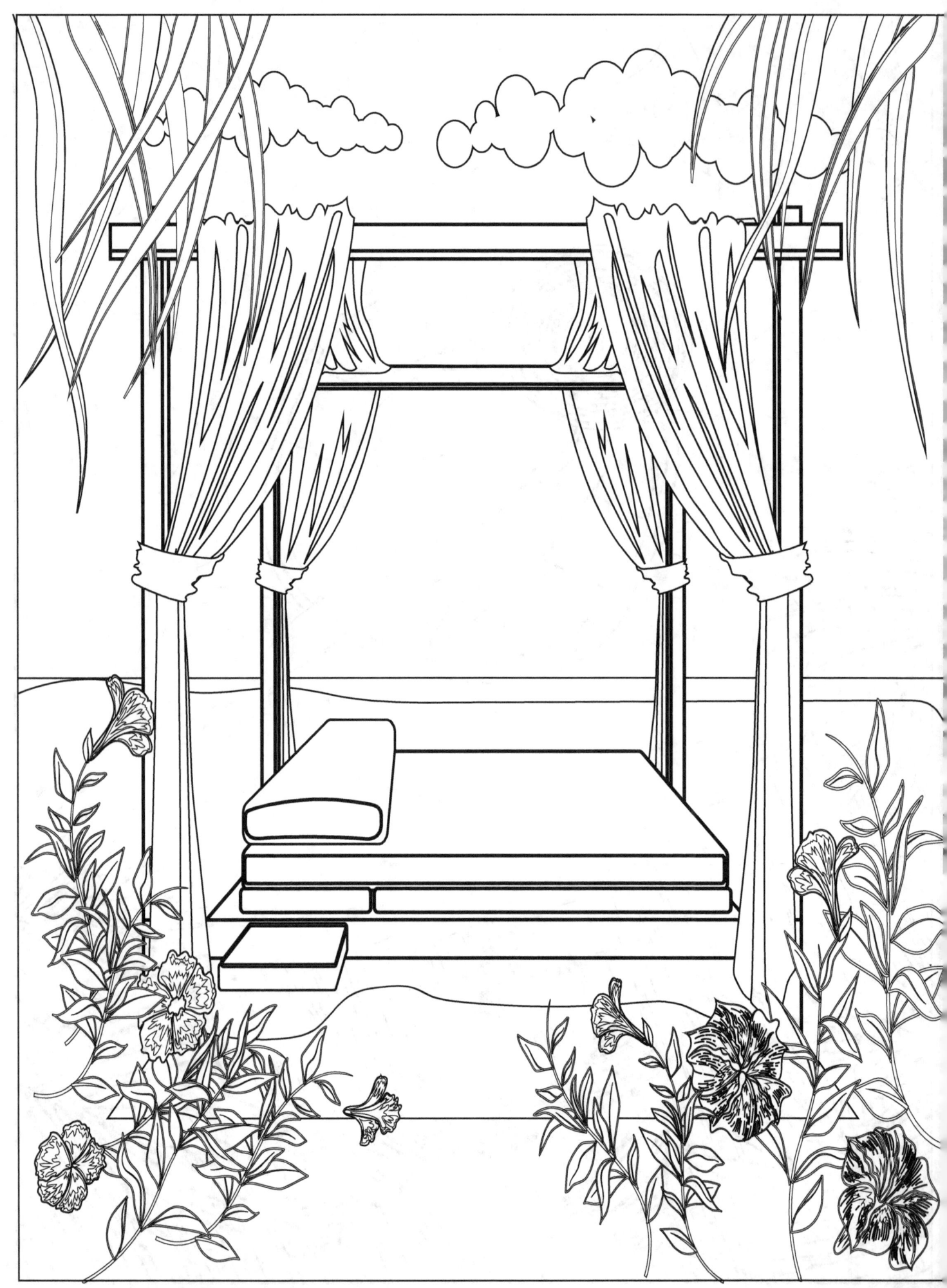

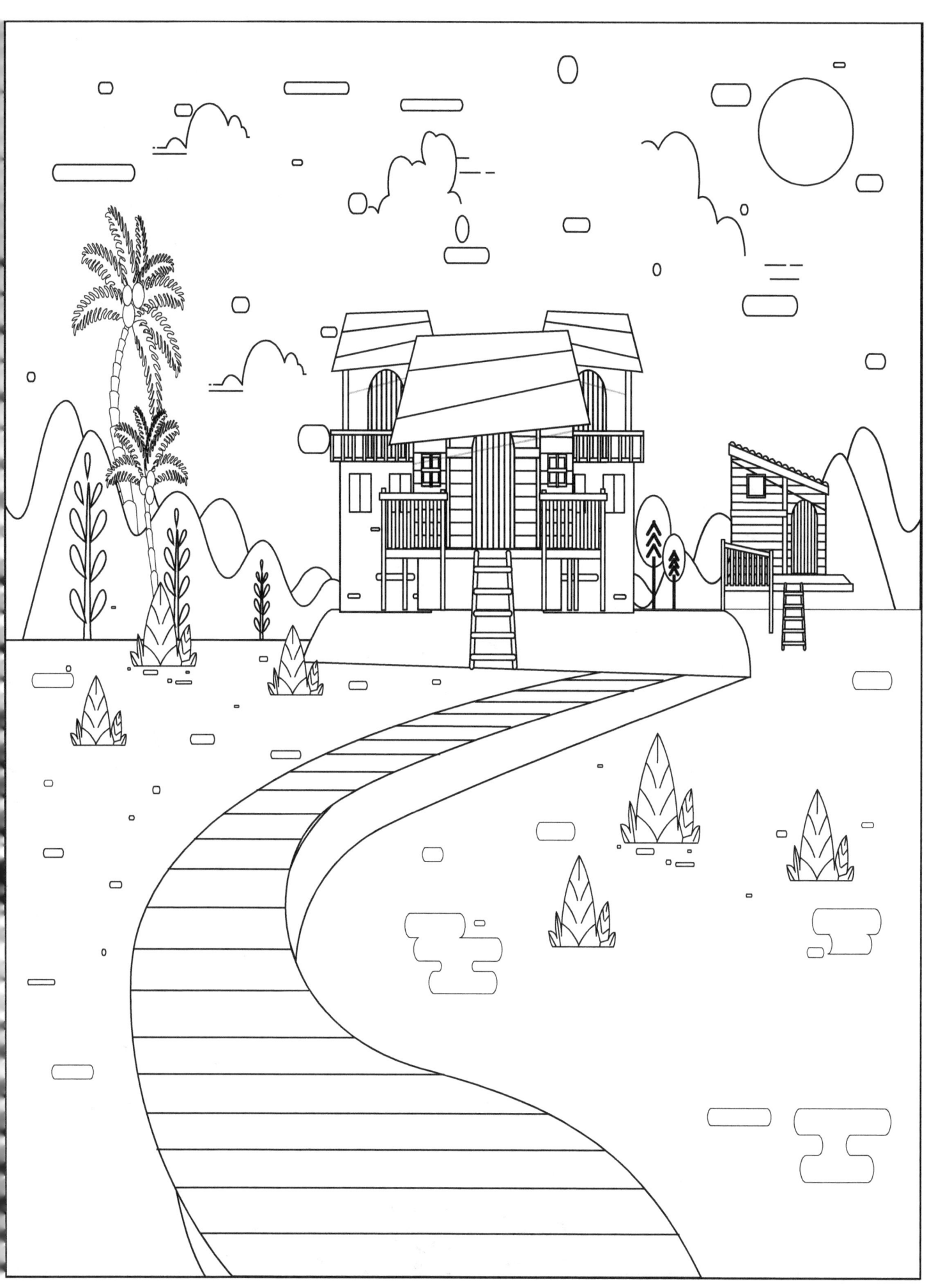

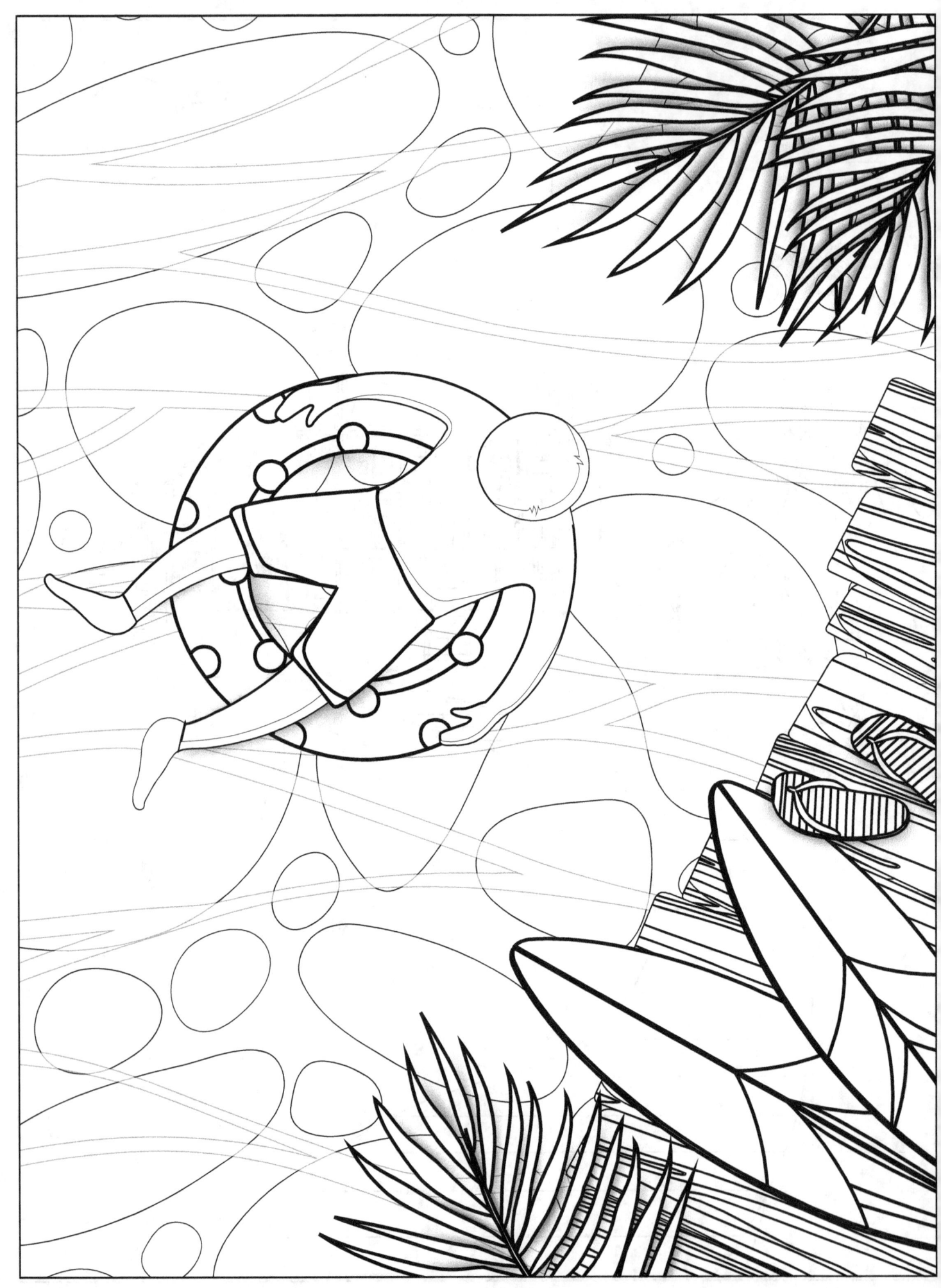

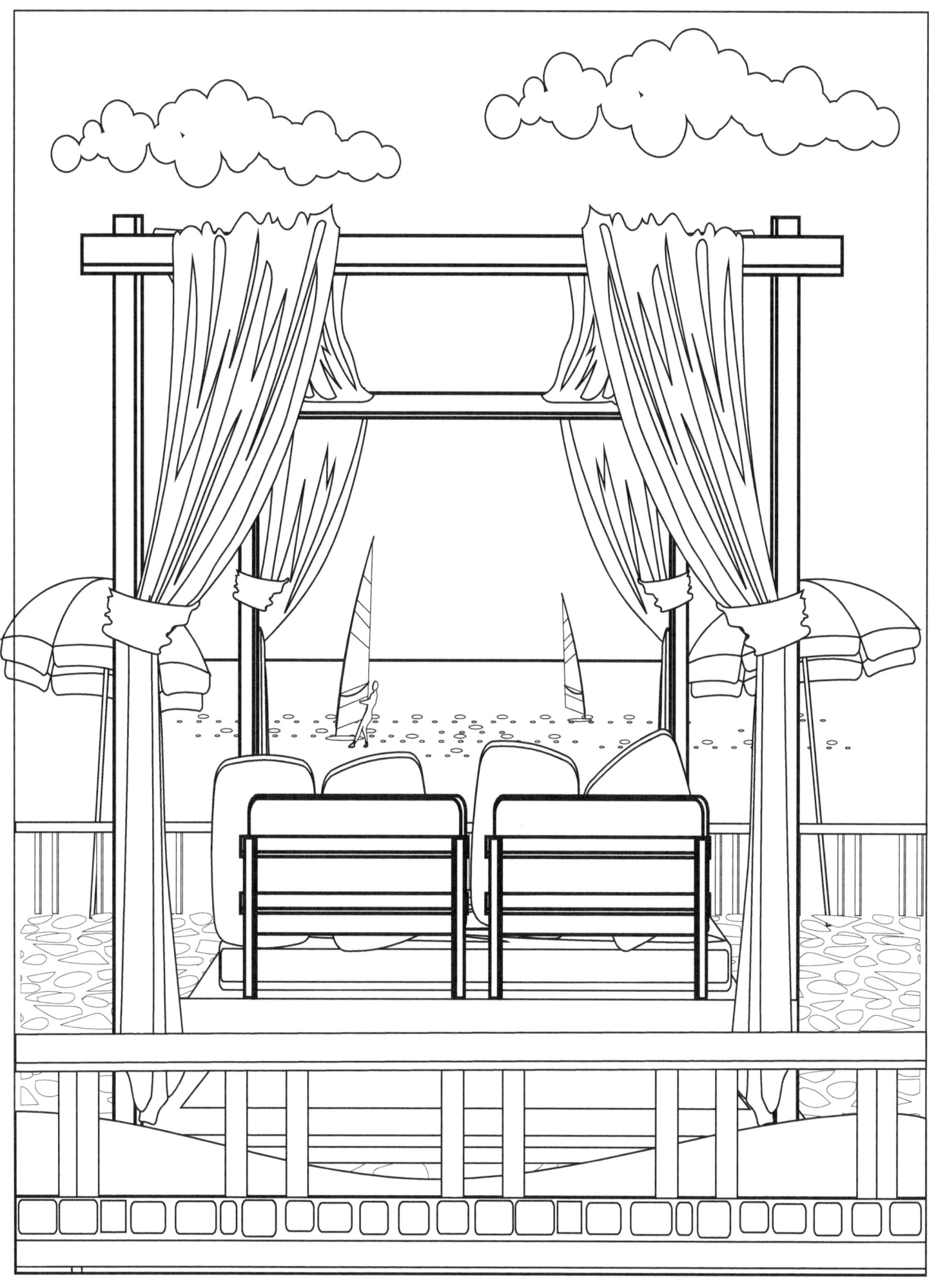

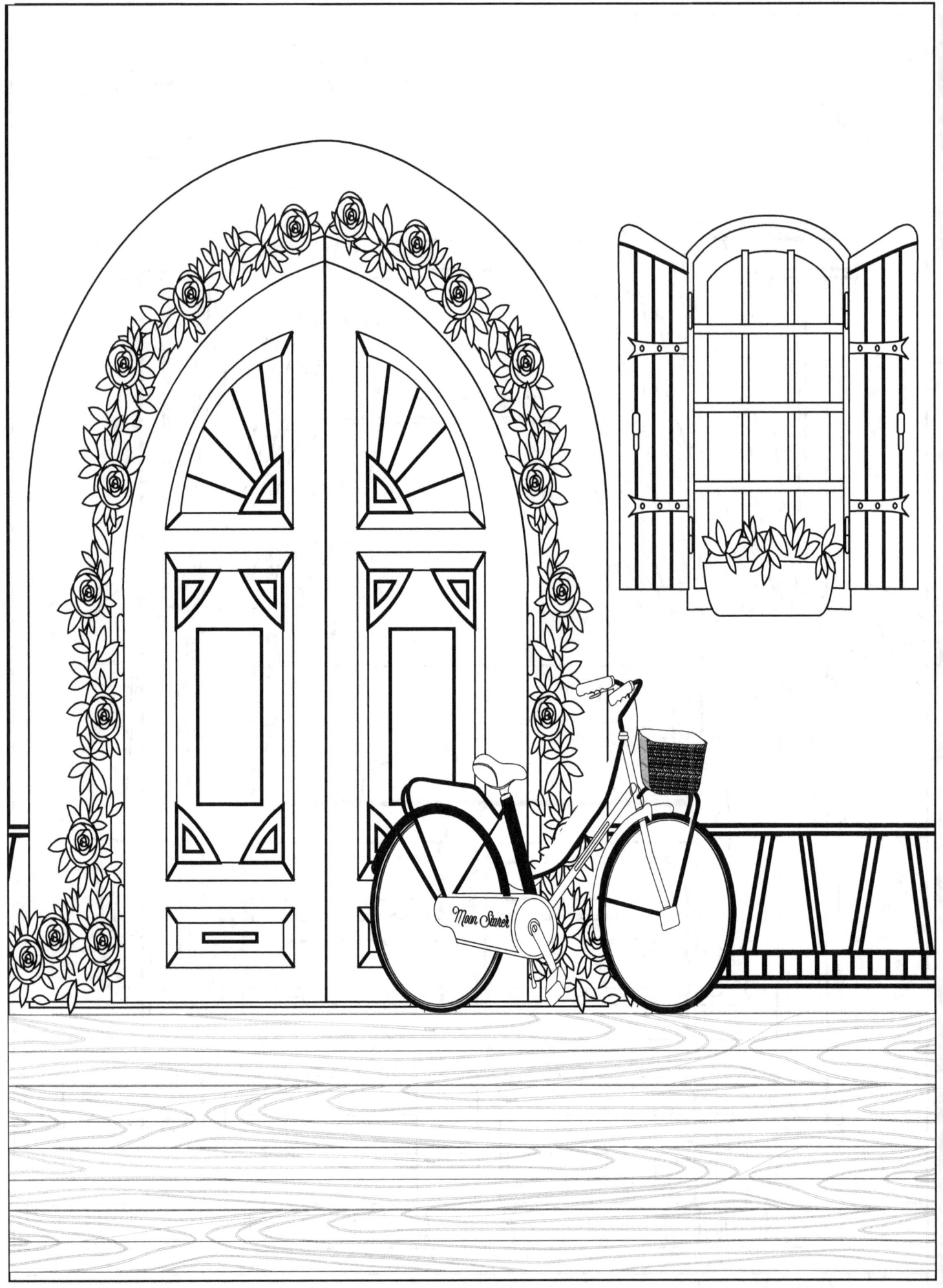

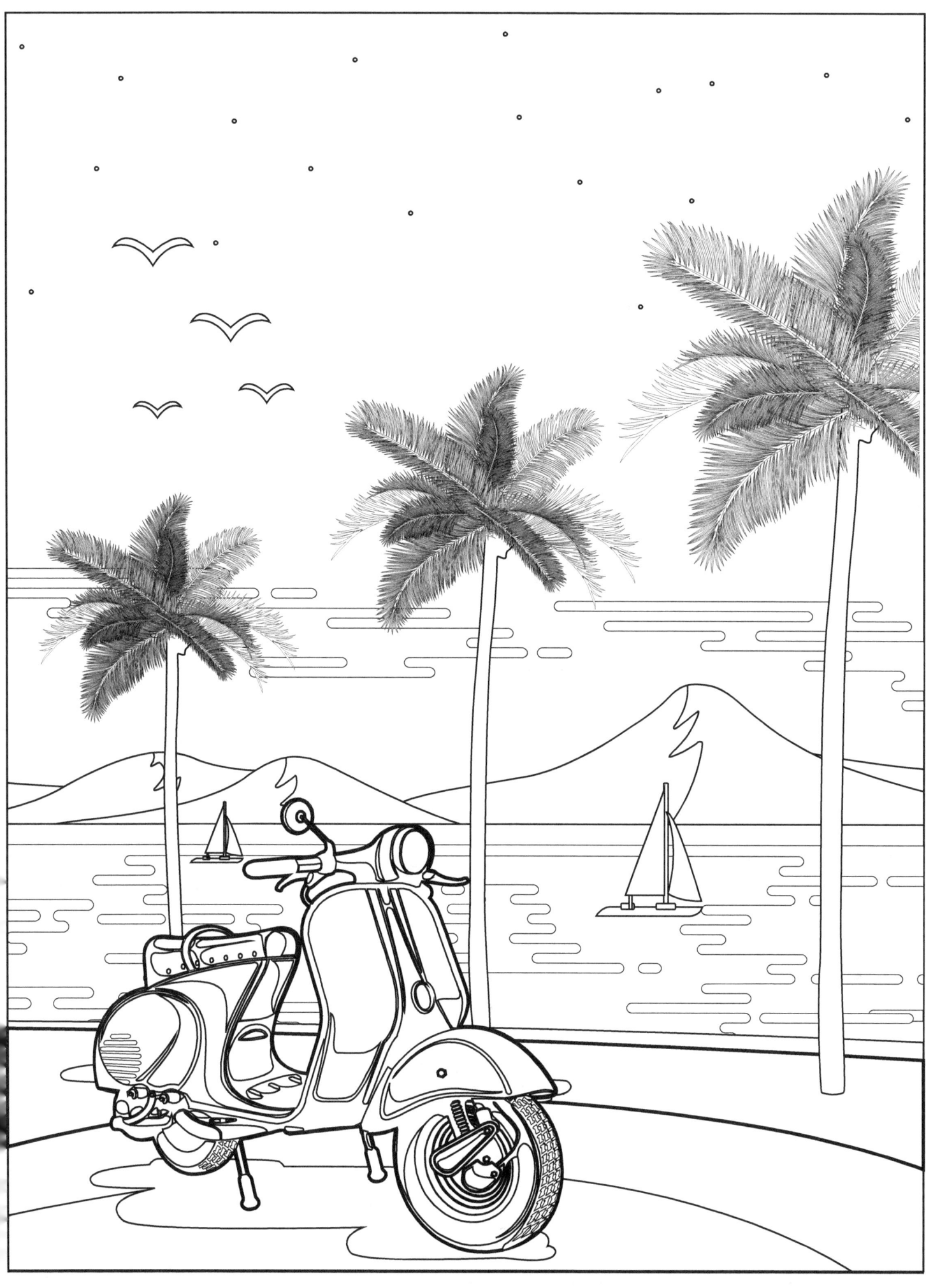

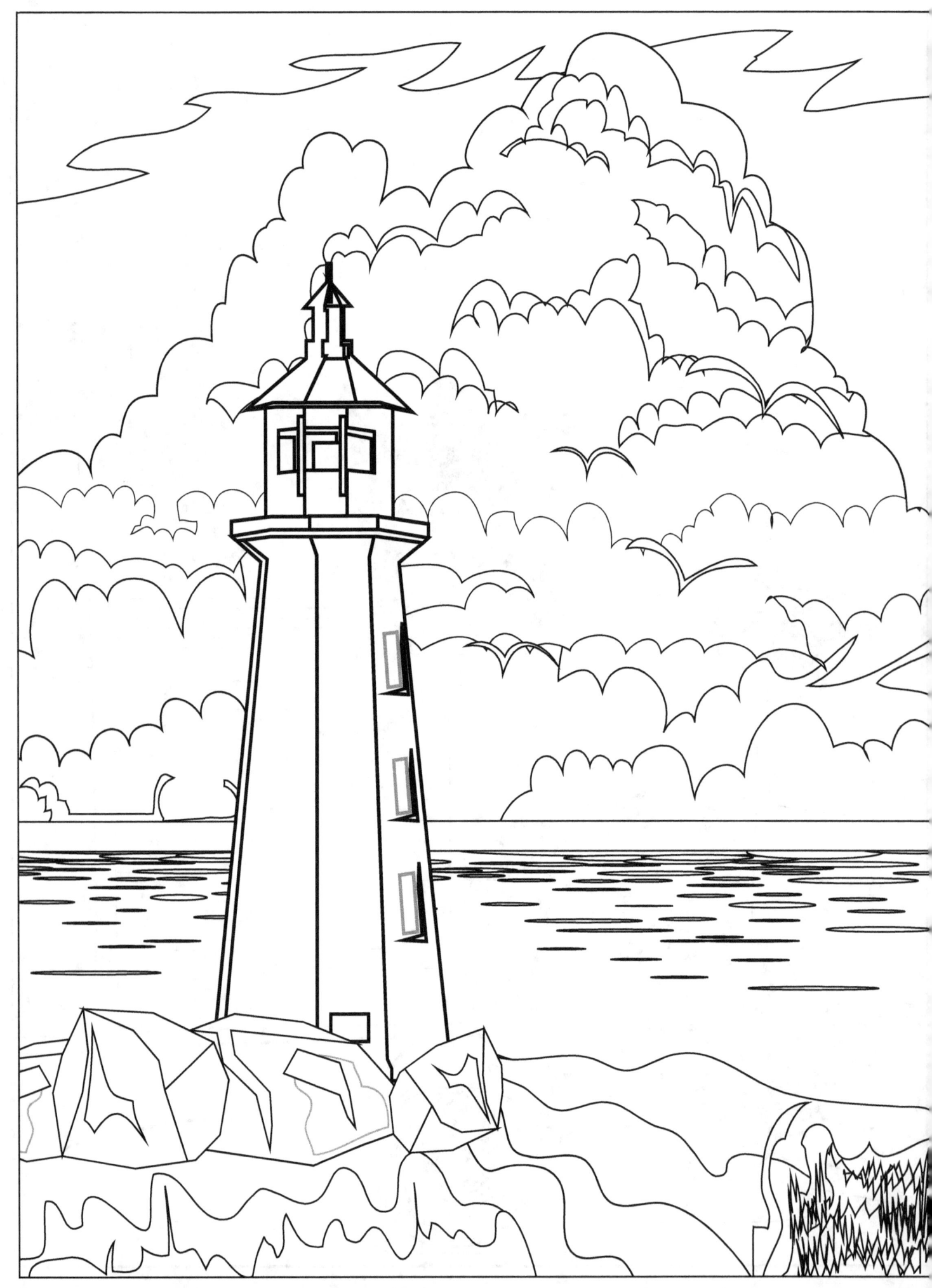

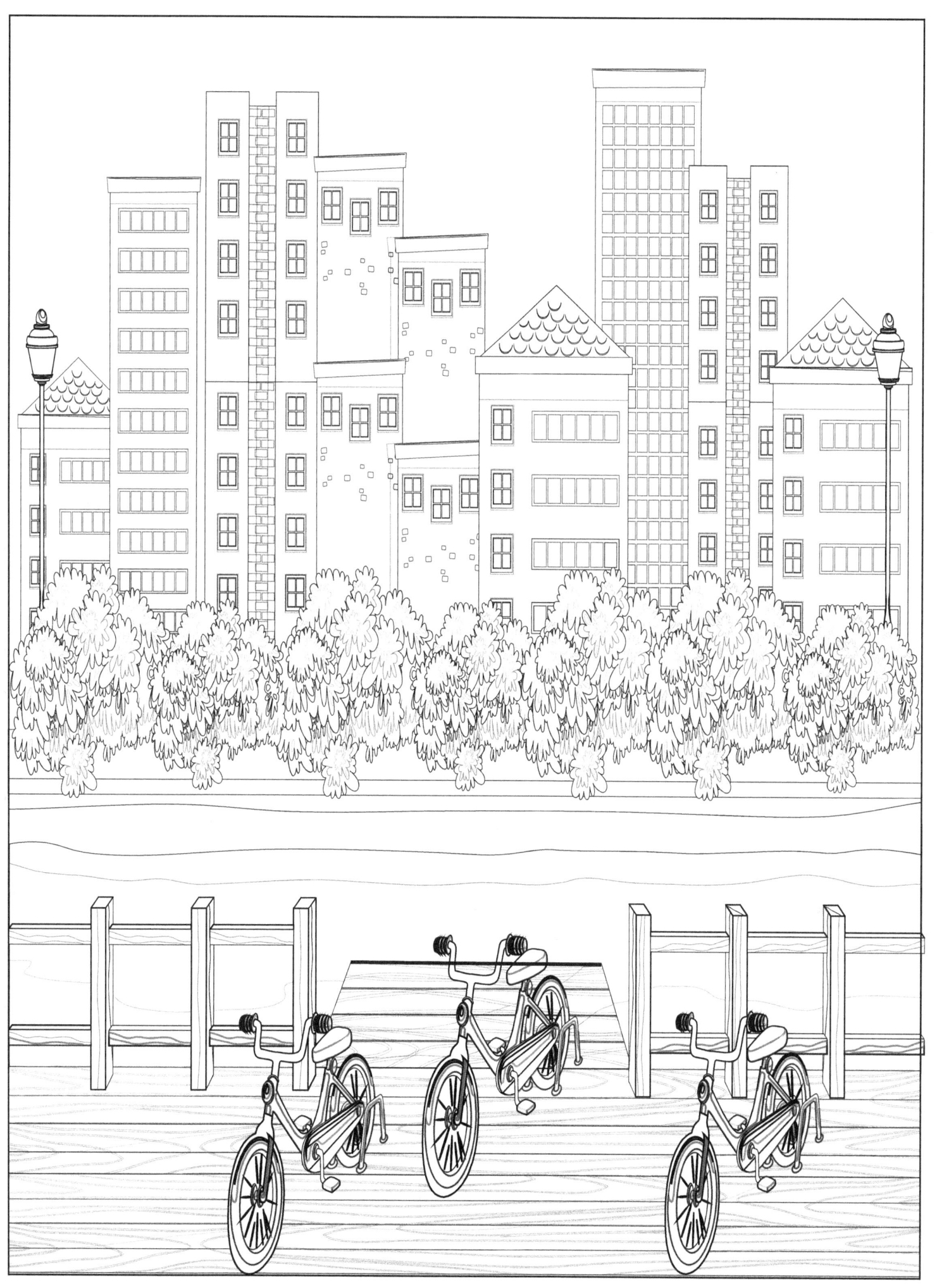

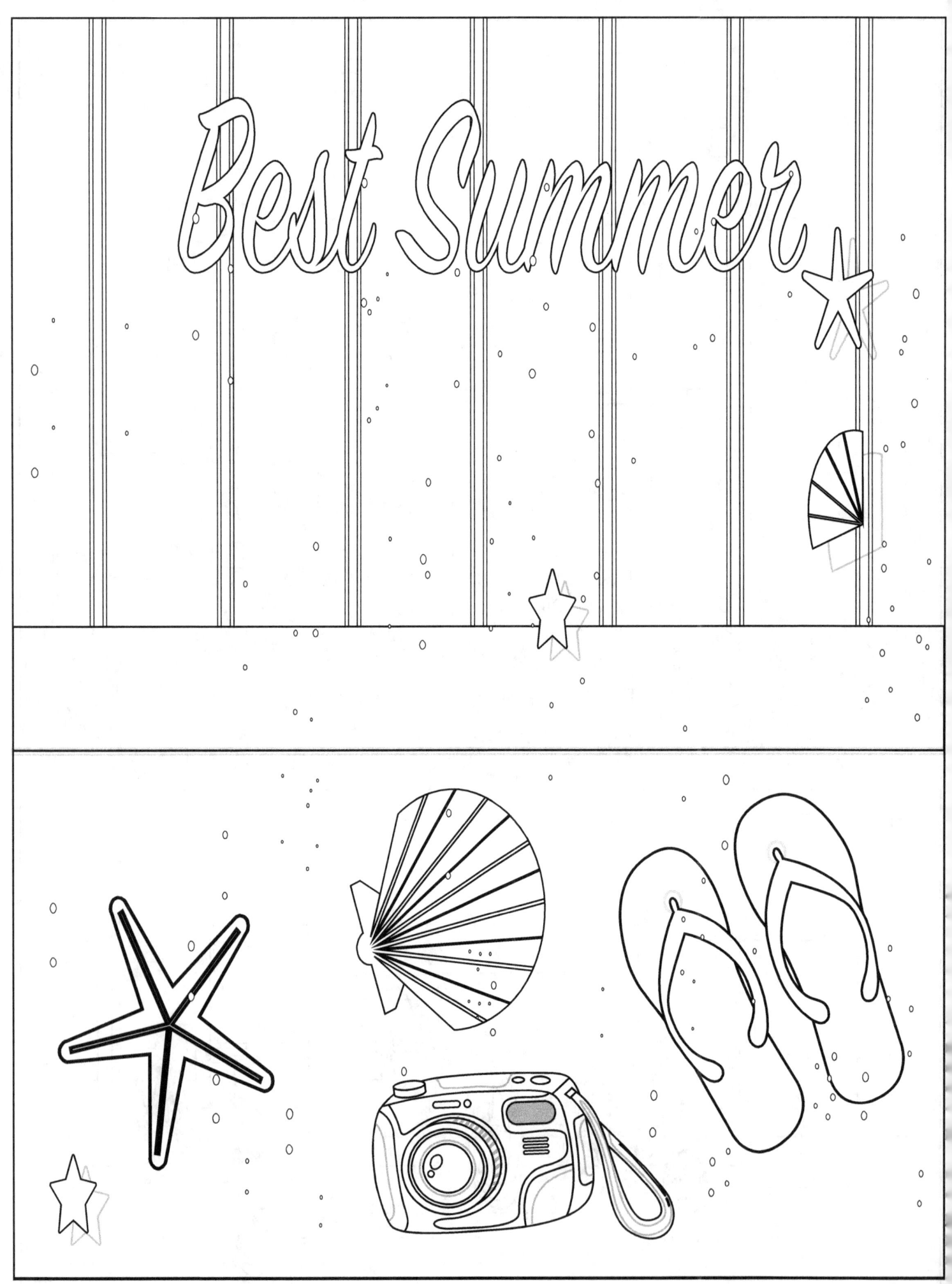

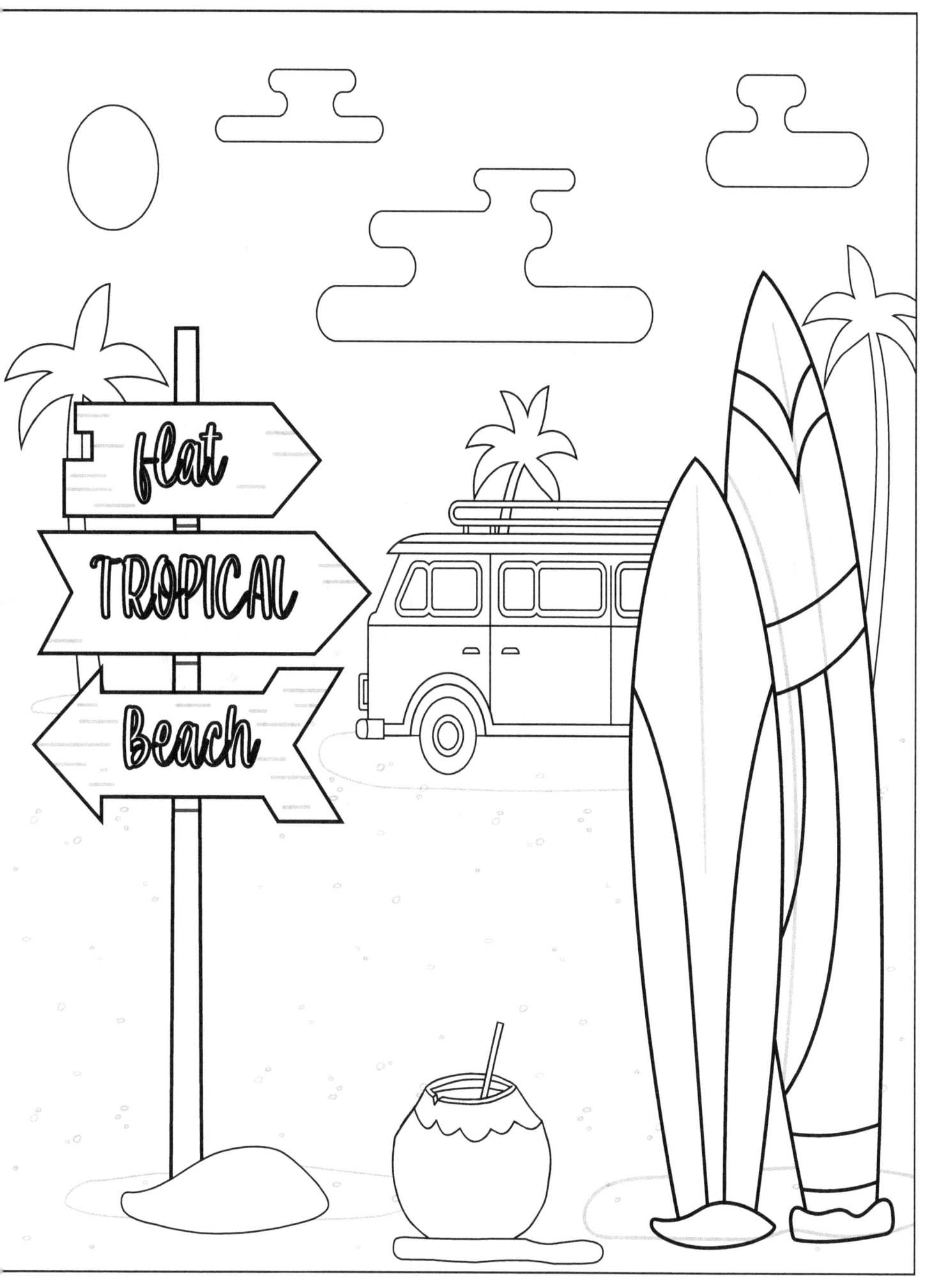

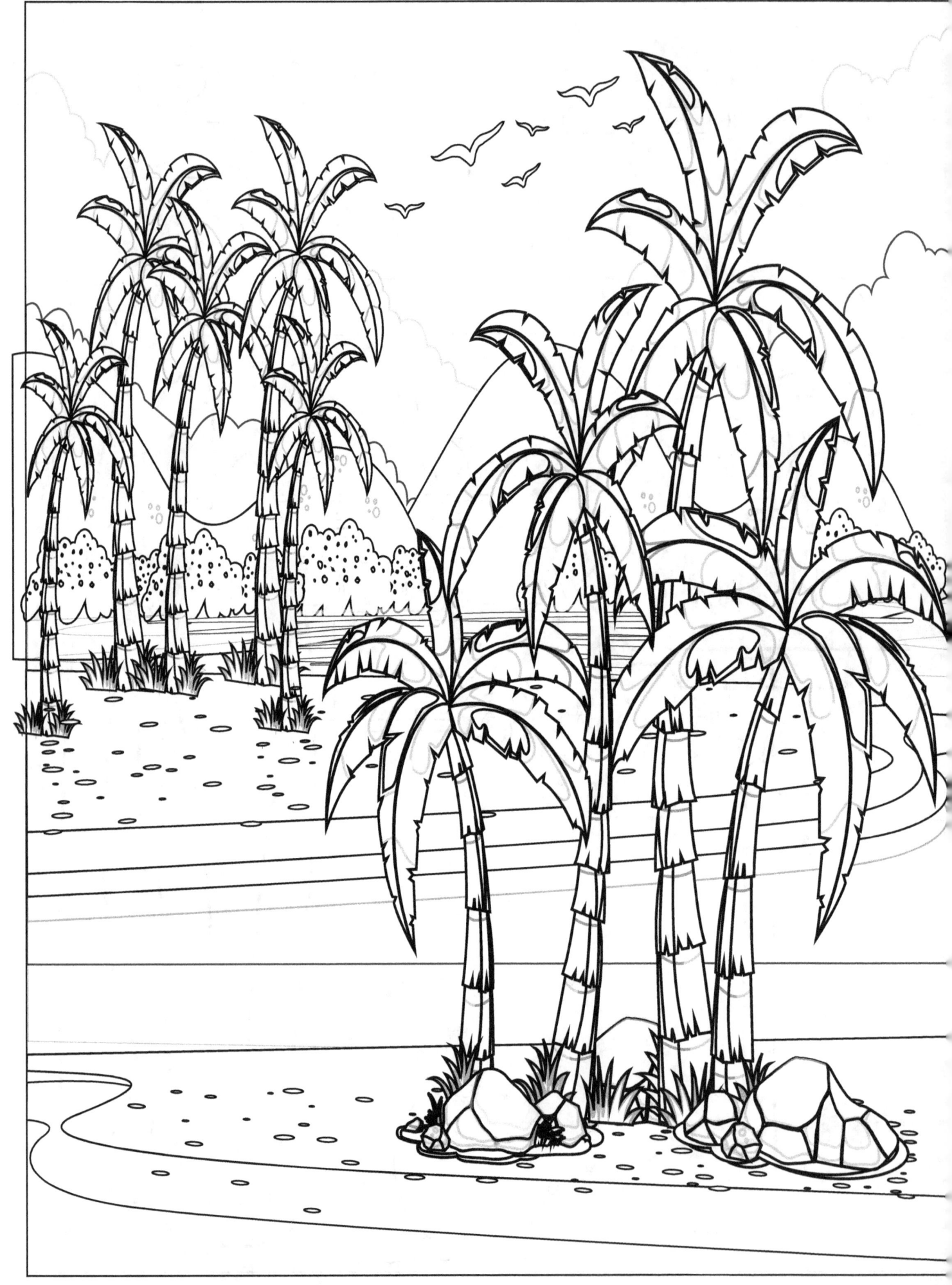

www.ingramcontent.com/pod-product-compliance
Lightning Source LLC
Chambersburg PA
CBHW080815220526
45466CB00011BB/3567